WHAT'S WRONG

Lynne Pettinger

First published in Great Britain in 2019 by

Policy Press
University of Bristol
1-9 Old Park Hill
Bristol
BS2 8BB
UK
t: +44 (0)117 954 5940
pp-info@bristol.ac.uk
www.policypress.co.uk

North America office:
Policy Press
c/o The University of Chicago Press
1427 East 60th Street
Chicago, IL 60637, USA
t: +1 773 702 7700
f: +1 773 702 9756
sales@press.uchicago.edu
www.press.uchicago.edu

© Policy Press 2019

British Library Cataloguing in Publication Data
A catalogue record for this book is available from the British Library.

Library of Congress Cataloging-in-Publication Data
A catalog record for this book has been requested.

ISBN 978-1-4473-4008-9 paperback
ISBN 978-1-4473-4103-1 ePub
ISBN 978-1-4473-4104-8 Mobi
ISBN 978-1-4473-4187-1 ePdf

Cover design by Lyn Davies
Printed and bound in Great Britain by TJ International,
Padstow
Policy Press uses environmentally responsible print
partners

What are the 21st century challenges shaping our lives today and in the future? At this time of social, political, economic and cultural disruption, this exciting series, published in association with the British Sociological Association, brings pressing public issues to the general reader, scholars and students. It offers standpoints to shape public conversations and a powerful platform for both scholarly and public debate, proposing better ways of understanding, and living in, our world.

Series Editors: Les Back, Goldsmiths, Pam Cox, University of Essex and Nasar Meer, University of Edinburgh

Other titles in this series:

Published

Miseducation by Diane Reay

Making sense of Brexit by Victor Seidler

Snobbery by David Morgan

What's wrong with work? by Lynne Pettinger

Forthcoming

Money by Mary Mellor – July 2019

"The world of work is changing rapidly, but established debates around the meaning, purpose and experience of work are not going away, while new questions are stimulated by the developments in green work, AI and robotics that are analysed here by Pettinger. This innovative book provides valuable groundings for modules dealing critically with everyday working lives, globalisation, culture and consumption."
Tracey Warren, University of Nottingham

"Combines a humanistic concern for workers with an evidence-based analysis of contemporary economic realities to show us a glimpse of work beyond capitalism. Essential reading for students of sociology and business alike."
Christopher Land, Anglia Ruskin University

Contents

About the author

Lynne Pettinger is an Associate Professor in Sociology at the University of Warwick. She is the author of *Work, consumption and capitalism* (Palgrave, 2015), and co-edited *A new sociology of work* (Blackwells, 2005). For more information, please see www.lynnepettinger.net

Acknowledgements

Dawn Lyon and Linsey McGoey gave gifts of time and enthusiasm in reading drafts, and I benefited enormously from their intellectual input and critique. Thanks so much, my friends. Thanks also to my anonymous reader for her kindness and insight. Thanks to Rebecca Tomlinson and Victoria Pittman at Policy Press.

Ian Brookes and Amy Hinterberger both offered intense encouragement and support.

Thanks to Rachel Cohen, Tracey Warren, Clare Lyonette, Vanessa Beck, Rebecca Taylor, Miriam Glucksmann, Diane Elson, Claire Blencowe, Ödül Bozkurt, Jo Littler, Eric Harrison, Humaira Chowdhury, Dave Hesmondhalgh, Simon Bell and Ewen Speed for helpful comments and conversations.

Thanks to Alba, Mercè, Janna, David, Theo, Aimee, Rod and others from the Three Ecologies and slow reading groups; Pam Cox offered initial enthusiasm and a sharp eye; John Narayan made suggestions on the race capitalism literature; Alice Mah took me to Brussels; Katherine Quinn did intense referencing work; Ros Burnley taught me about horticulture. I owe replies to Rich Davis and Phil Mizen and a present to Brian Pettinger.

I have had a permanent job and a period of study leave to write this book. Thanks to John Solomos, and to my other colleagues in the Sociology Department at Warwick. The British Academy funded research into green jobs, an anonymous NHS trust funded research into healthcare technologies. Thanks to Ewen and Andy for the latter.

Andrew Goffey has given freely of his knowledge of Stengers' ideas, and of software, and never stops being clever and kind.

List of tables

List of abbreviations

ASEAN	Association of Southeast Asian Nations
BPO	Business process outsourcing
CAD	Computer-aided design
CIS	Communications and information systems
CMT	Cut, make, trim
CSR	Corporate social responsibility
EDSAC	Electronic delay storage automatic computer
ENIAC	Electronic numerical integrator and computer
EPOS	Electronic points of sale
EPR	Electronic patient record
ERP	Enterprise resource planning
EU	European Union
EWI	Employing workers indicator
GFA	Global Framework Agreement
GMO	Genetically modified organism
GP	General practitioner
GPN	Global production network
HE	Higher education
ICD	International Classification of Diseases
ICT	Information and communications technology
ILO	International Labour Organization
IMF	International Monetary Fund
ITUC	International Trade Union Confederation
LDC	Less developed countries
LPT	Labour process theory
MBA	Master of Business Administration
NGO	Non-governmental organisation
NPM	New public management
OPS	Office productivity software
QWL	Quality of working life
SEZ	Special economic zone
TINA	There is No Alternative

TNC	Transnational corporation
UN	United Nations
UNEP	United Nations Environment Programme

Part One

ONE

Framing the present: capitalism, work and crisis

What's wrong with work?

Sample dialogue from my life:

> What's your book called?
> 'What's wrong with work?' It's about the ethics and
>   politics of how work is changing at the moment.
> Good title. You should talk to my partner, who's an
>   XXX [insert name of almost any job].

> What's your book called?
> 'What's wrong with work?'
> That's going to be a long book.

> What's your book called?
> 'What's wrong with work?' It's about...
> How long have you got? I hate my job, I hate my
>   boss, I hate the customers.

If ever a book title was an invitation to grumble, one that asks the question 'What's wrong with work?' is it. Someone once answered 'I don't have a couch in my office', but I think they were joking. Answering a question like 'What's wrong with work?' could well involve writing a list, as that's a normal way to provide answers. I wish it were that easy. In the course of the book I will open out ways of thinking about ethics and

3

politics of current work for the lifeworld of workers and for how work contributes to making the world. The task of providing an account of the problem of work is pretty difficult, given the complexities of different kinds of work, of variations across time and space, and because of the many different elements that might be important when thinking about good and bad jobs, which may easily contradict each other (for example, routines generate stability but also boredom; working with customers brings pleasure as well as pain). Further, the conceptual tools that could help – work, economy, and ethics – are not straightforward; it's hard even to know what questions to ask.

What kind of person sets a question for a book to answer knowing that it is not answerable? An idiot, maybe. But being an idiot is no bad thing. Idiots serve the function of interrupting what is common sense, what is taken for granted[1] often by asking naïve questions. Questions don't necessarily have answers, or solutions. Sometimes they are useful because they pose a problem differently. It might also be that questions that get asked in a book don't find answers there (or in any other book), but in practices. That seems important. By the end of this book you might not have an answer to the big question of 'What is to be done?' I would settle for offering a different take on what the problems are. In working towards understanding the question of 'What's wrong with work?', I am asking three other, naïve, questions.

Q1 How is work organised?

This question asks for understanding of things like the contracts that are offered to workers, how and how much they are paid, how they are recruited, trained and managed, how they are able to negotiate and bargain with employers, what technologies they use and the whole array of factors that might influence how people experience work. This question frames many, many existing ways of thinking about what's wrong with work. It is a question that is there in political disputes over the right way to treat workers, in collective bargaining, in corporate decision-making, in policy-making. It is also at the heart of existing ways of thinking about the ethics of work: of decent work, of dignity at work, and of job quality; of reducing the pains and dangers of work. Answers take different forms, and commonly include developing standards to use in measuring and assessing job quality; developing regulations to control abuse; and developing political actions for campaigning for better work. It matters in so many ways, but I think it works best when asked alongside two other questions.

Q2 How are different kinds of work interconnected?

The assumption that work means paid work means that political and ethical responses to the question of 'What's wrong with work?' then focus on paid work. Recognition is a political act. So defining work as paid work has political effects. It produces exclusions, denies the importance of some activities and privileges others. Question 2 challenges that assumption by asking what counts as work, and how different kinds of work relate to each other.

It might seem that this would mean losing the analytic value of work defined as paid work, or of assuming that *everything* is work. I find that daft. As long as it's clear why and how an activity is defined as work, and what the analytic purpose of that is, then it seems reasonable to me. Paid work is one way of organising work; it relies on other kinds of work. The connections and dependencies between different ways that work is organised are really important to understanding the ethics and politics of contemporary work. Thinking about the many forms taken by the informal economy across the world (see Chapter Six), and as feminist scholars studying work and life have discussed, most work isn't a career, or even a job. It's what gets done to make life possible. It's care work, provisioning work, informal exchange of home-produced goods. It's voluntary work and domestic work. It's forced work and slavery, prison labour and welfare-to-work. It's even the prosumption ('production through consumption') and co-creation attached to leisure and lifestyle activities. It's gig work and forced self-employment, in which case it's paid but without the normal extras of a job: employment contracts, employment rights and state regulation. These kinds of work might relate to, contribute to and depend on paid work in various ways, but they are neither reducible to paid work, nor lesser than it. I am indebted here to many other feminist writers in making these arguments.[2]

In asking this question I have two aims. One is to recognise work and make it visible. The second is to understand how work in one time and place is reliant, in complicated ways, on many other kinds of work. From paid work that relies on unpaid care, to automated tasks that rely on a software engineer's understanding of doing a task, to the dependence of a garment worker's livelihood on brand executives' decisions, work is interconnected across times and places. By exploring these two issues it starts to be possible to see that paying attention to the problems of some kinds of (paid) work can hide from notice the problems of other kinds of work.

Q3 What does work do?

I don't think this question is asked enough. That might be because it's ridiculously extensive, given that work is so diverse and complex – the obvious retort should be another question 'What work are you talking about, Lynne?' If the ethics of work pertains mostly to the experiences of the worker (as in Q1) or to the interdependencies between kinds of work (Q2), then asking about the effects of work is redundant and wasted. Many of the ways of conceptualising workers see them as powerless in the face of capitalism, managerial demands and neoliberal ways of being. Where that logic dominates, then the idea of work having effects in the world, the idea that work makes realities, seems odd because it appears to be saying that workers are powerful – which is hard to imagine if they are also exploited.

Work has effects on those who do it. Bodies are changed, feelings are made, social relations are made and changed. Often, the effects of work on the worker are framed either as questions of avoiding exploitation or of creating meaningful work. I think that sets the ethical focus too precisely and two further ways of thinking about work extend the agenda considerably.

Asking 'What does work do?' is a way of thinking about economic practices as actively made in many different ways.

That is, of positioning work as immanent to economic practices. Work is not a given, something that just falls out of economics ready-made. It is a series of practices that produce, create, alter and affect life. One obvious way in which work has practical effects can be seen in the way that the work of technological expertise creates the possibilities for other kinds of work. In designing tools and techniques, in setting policies, many kinds of expertise produce realities. They make some practices easy and others hard, and they reproduce their assumptions in the tools and norms to which they contribute. Understanding what work does and what it makes it possible to do is therefore central to thinking about what's wrong with work.

Other work too is involved in this making of reality, often work that is invisible or deleted (see Chapter Three for more). The ethical implications of how work gets done emerge when the manner of doing the work affects what it does. So doing something with care or carelessly matters. The ethics of what work does in the world are on display in such cases. It is especially obvious in relation to work directly on or with others, whether service for a client, care for a parent, or negotiation with a colleague. Ethics broadens out from the effect of work on the worker, to the effects on those humans and non-humans that are imbricated in that activity. My interest in the politics of the everyday means questioning the inevitability of what work and life are like. The effects of work on the world include causing and repairing damage, to nature, to humans, to other kinds of matter.

Building the questions

These three questions have been on my mind as I have written this book. They are obviously interconnected and answering one often contributes to a greater understanding of another. Negotiations between brokers, for example, affect which company gets a contract to produce, what the margins are, who gets squeezed, how the work will be organised and how the workers will be treated.

The present is an opportune time to extend and enhance conversations about the ethics and politics of work, the quality of jobs, about how paid and unpaid work make life possible, and about work in relation to other kinds of work. In the rest of this chapter, I'll show the reasoning behind these three questions and explain the ideas that help me to find ways of answering them, in order to find some insight into that overarching and complicated question of 'What's wrong with work?' that I am exploring here. I'll start by describing the present, a time of distressing crisis and conflict. The present time must be understood in relation to environmental catastrophe, seemingly unstoppable technological change, and unstable, unpredictable everyday life. These phenomena matter to the long-lasting present, although they are often thought about in relation to what the future might bring. The next section describes 'capitalocentrism', a concept that is one of the building blocks of my argument about how to understand work in relation to the rest of life. Then I describe my other building block, a way of thinking about ethics as part of the 'worthless rock' of everyday life. These twin blocks are the theories on which my later arguments rely.

What's wrong with now?

I miss being able to believe in progress. I am not sure when I gave up on progress: maybe it was the financial crisis of 2008, or perhaps it was a few years after, when the knot of financial, political and corporate sectors had clearly tied itself up again more tightly than ever; perhaps it was the resurgence of right-wing politics across the globe, and the crackdowns on democracy that followed popular uprisings such as those seen in the Arab Spring. Perhaps it has a longer history, based in knowledge of the fragility of movements towards protecting workers' rights, or towards global social equality. It has certainly been affected by learning to rethink assumptions that linear progress is possible. Bubbling under, always, is a sense of a crisis with a different kind of temporality, a different presence in the social world: the crisis of nature, the geological force of ozone depletion, biodiversity loss, chemical pollution, nitrogen cycle interference and – famously – climate change. Isabelle Stengers writes that we live 'in catastrophic times'[3] marked by a compelling environmental crisis that results from the 'intrusion of Gaia', the return with a vengeance of a nature that the western human world had thought it could dominate or at least contain.

While the political crises, crises of war and poverty, and crises of work capture media attention, what is really biting us is that environmental catastrophe which we seem unwilling to see. Reading the opinions of those whom Stengers calls 'Our Guardians': the technocrats, politicians, the mainstream media, though, it would seem that there is no crisis – not of capitalism, politics, or anything else: the 2008 financial crisis has subsided, business in the financial districts continues, the global elite carry on with tax avoidance schemes and with promoting economic policies that reduce tax burden in the name of investment. It's business as usual. Climate change denial persists, austerity policies are institutionalised, and despite years of campaigning, everyday working lives are often marked by struggle, poor treatment and insecurity. We have to keep going like this, Our Guardians tell us, because of TINA: There Is No Alternative. What kind of world is it, where the migrant workers building stadia for global sport events like the football World Cup do so on indentured contracts, and deaths due to falls and accidents in the absence of effective safety measures are public knowledge but publicly ignored? Only a world in crisis can push for economic growth in the face of environmental catastrophe, and can claim global belonging through sport on the back of elite corruption and the deaths of migrant workers.

A crisis is a specific, dangerous moment in time – a tipping point, if you like. It comes with all kinds of feelings: maybe you share some of my fear and panic. For Déborah Danowski and Eduardo Viveiros de Castro,[4] western fears for the end of the world come as 'modernity starts to implode before our very eyes', as realisation dawns that economic reasoning and human domination are nothing in the face of the long, slow geological catastrophe. 'Now' is a time of catastrophe. Now is formed by histories of industrialisation, colonialism, love of technology, domination of nature. The catastrophe of now is a result of political, social, environmental and economic violence. We know inequalities are deeply entrenched; we know economists' orthodoxies are stubborn like weeds. The catastrophes of now

– the resurgence of political extremism, the deepening of inequalities and the slow–quick–slow rhythm of violent climate change – are often 'explained' with reference to an apparently dominant form of capitalism, neoliberalism. The complexity of concrete effects doesn't always match the abstract noun, the fuzzy concept that gets applied. The unnameable gets named, and so becomes more real than reality.

The usual explanation for the catastrophe of environmental crisis is the zombie persistence of capitalism, and of its most devilish form, neoliberalism. Sad and scary stories are common in the social sciences, where spending days engaged in the problems with the world 'from a critical perspective' create cynicism and negativity. Critique, endless critique, participates in producing the sense that There Is No Alternative, this time with the tag line 'because everything is always and everywhere rubbish' (or similar). If critique was so powerful as a way of generating change, then academics would rule of the world. We don't, though. So I'll make a lower-key promise: how can I ask good questions to find new possibilities for change?

Knots and knotty problems

Simple critiques of complicated problems are not enough. The interwoven complications have to be thought through. Three features of contemporary life have a particularly strong effect on the present: the constantly present, if not always visible, processes of informal work; the dangerous promises of technologisation; and the inferno of environmental catastrophe. In Part Two, I'll focus on each of these in turn. They are not so much cases of the kind that make for convenient 'case studies'. Rather, they are what Tim Ingold calls knots,[5] tied into other phenomena, part of the meshwork of life. Each is part of the other, and of the other phenomena I study (work, economic activity) but never reducible to one or other of those. They are often discussed in terms of the future (coming together in 'end of work' scenarios, where technological substitution of human effort might make possible less paid work and less consumption, which will be environmentally beneficial and make household work equitable). These are knots that matter now, made by the twisting and tangling of multiple threads. They have to be taken seriously to understand contemporary work.

Technology

Technologies are diverse and numerous. I am especially interested in IT and in the software on which it relies. Headlines that refer to the fear and promise of robots replacing human jobs are a dramatic illustration of the more mundane processes through which work is being and will be altered by software, including platforms such as Amazon web services. Software reshapes existing forms of work, for example, the growth of 'off-shore' business processing, the facilitation of long supply chains through complex logistical software operations, and the reshaping of medical care with computer-aided diagnostic tools. As such, software has a politics and an ethics that is not always fully articulated[6] even as it is both worked on, and affects others. Change, often poorly understood, is re-described as disruption, or even less meaningfully, as disruptive innovation.

Not all technologies are shiny, much is mundane. Simple fuel-efficient stove technologies radically change how much domestic labour women do.[7] The knot of technology encounters the knots of environment and of informal work in this example. That is because 'technology' is not an abstract, distinct force, but always connected and entangled. 'Socio-technology' is the ugly word used to describe this interplay between technology and social relations. What are the mundane ways, the subtle and scarcely visible ways, that changes in software and hardware are altering work?

Environment

Western assumptions about nature have long made it seem that nature is a (free) resource for human use, as a source of value, secondary in its importance in comparison to human life. 'Nature' here refers to non-human life forms, including plants and animals, geological features, including oil, gas and coal, and those elements essential for other life (for example, water, oxygen, nutrition). A diverse range of elements are fitted into this category 'nature', with different geographies and temporalities (from a dragonfly to the lifespan of a mountain). In particular, nature gets imagined as a resource for capitalist accumulation, whether as raw materials for extraction, as sunshine that generates electricity, soil for growing, or a place too cold or too hot. It is the unspoken base of capitalist activity, and work of many kinds is involved in manipulating, extracting, monitoring and even repairing it. The rendering of nature as open to exploitation to human culture is an example of the dualistic quality of western thinking that separates and generates hierarchies between entities that might be better understood as co-dependent.

Environmental crises are affecting population movements, agriculture, housing, consumption and, of course, work: all the stuff of daily life, the visible and invisible work of existence. There are and will be more struggles over rights and resources. Current policy responses are limited by desperate attempts to maintain economic growth via the tried and tested 'business as usual' tools, despite the stupidities this involves. How is work affected by climate change? How can tensions between keeping traditional jobs and environmental protection be managed? What kinds of work are needed to ameliorate the effects of climate change? How can the tension between work that does good but damages those who do it be considered? This knot is entangled with technology. Narratives of progress of human lives rely on the fairy tale of technological innovation as a means to solve problems. And that the development of technology is connected very strongly to the ideology of growth. Green technology offers the distant promise of geo-engineering; economic science is offering sustainable development and a green economy. At this point, it's worth remembering that green isn't just the colour of nature and eco-happiness, but of mould and poisons. As with technology, it isn't useful to render 'nature' or 'environment' as a bounded, separate force: 'nature' means 'socio-nature'. Another ugly but useful phrase.

Everyday life

Socio-nature and socio-technology are terms that indicate diffuse and interconnected relations across domains that are normally considered apart. The 'socio' part is the third knot, which takes seriously the ordinariness and indeterminate banality of everyday life. Here it means noticing those objects, relations and practices that are so taken for granted that they scarcely register as relevant for thinking about work. They have to be deliberately brought to mind. Ideas about everyday life invite focus on the routines and objects that are important to the experience of living. I have also already mentioned that not all work is paid work in the formal sector: with a contract, with a wage, with set hours of work. There's an awful lot of work-like activity that is not paid, but that makes life possible. This includes the estimated 60+ per cent of all work activity that is not formal work.[8] It includes the work needed to care for the very young and the very old. It includes the routine maintenance of the tools necessary to do work, from getting fuel for the stove to updating computer software. Thinking about these activities and practices changes the shape of the question about 'What's wrong with work?', and asks for different kinds of answers. It weaves work into everyday life.

What's wrong with economics?

These three questions and three knots are my way into answering a question as big as 'What's wrong with work?' My argument relies on the concept of 'capitalocentrism' – the idea that explanations of the world that only notice economic activity are limited.

For all kinds of economic thinkers, and in many kinds of communication – from news bulletins to Nobel Prize Committees, to anti-capitalist pamphlets – the categories of 'economy', 'economics', 'markets' and 'capitalism' tend to be treated as though they are real, definable and distinguishable entities. But they are not; they are actively made in real times and spaces, through the actions of policies, people, technologies and materials. They are simultaneously legal, social and cultural as well as economic. Simplified theories and the common shortcuts – the abstractions – of ordinary speech hide this contingency and variability. The con of 'economy' is to pose as a master category, outside of social, political, natural and cultural spheres, that it is a natural entity. But this is a political achievement that makes it possible to address 'the economy' as a beast that has its own demands that must be appeased, no matter the impact. It collapses the differences between economic theories and the operation of specific kinds of economic activity.

When 'The Economy' is treated as a thing in itself, a real thing, then economic policy appears just as a technocratic intervention that simply must happen given the nature of markets, and then it seems that there is no alternative. Then we see what Isabelle Stengers[9] calls 'the infernal alternatives' becoming entrenched across a series of practices. A whole range of assumptions by economic sciences, including that markets create efficient outcomes and that people make self-interested decisions, go into making that seem natural. Zombie economics relies on metaphors derived from dated readings of natural sciences, and is especially fascinated by metaphors that ally economies with machines.[10] It hides the normativity of its reasoning, and claims normative outcomes are natural. It denies its own social resonance.

In case you hadn't guessed, I don't accept this understanding of what economic activity is. I do not see 'The Economy' as given, natural and inevitable, but rather as actively produced by specific acts, by policies, knowledges and technologies, through beliefs and decisions about how economies do and should work, even as ordinary people are encouraged to feel powerless as 'governance' by technocratic rationality seems to move closer to replacing democracy.[11] Instead, I think people, ideas, technologies, natures and other entities assemble economic activity, which is contingent and complicated. So that must mean that how science, expertise and knowledge about economics gets made, and how political and business decisions are made, matters to the shape and form of economic activity. And, crucially, that any claim about how economic activity operates contains within it normative claims, as Albert Hirschman[12] showed so well. Economies are affected by ideas about what an economy is and how it operates; what markets are and how they should operate. To put it another way, 'The Economy' is not just a container, an abstract 'form' within which economic activity happens. It is made through and formed *as* work (among other things), including, but not only, the work of economists. A key argument in this book is that economies are made, not given.

Capitalism's multiplicities

Capitalism is an (always evolving) history and a theory of how economic life is organised and entwined in social life. It relies on markets where property rights for goods and services are exchanged for money, under conditions of market competition, and with the pursuit of profit as the aim.[13] Simple definitions, though, have their limits. This one doesn't say much about how these goods and services are made and used. I consider capitalism to be a vast assemblage of social, cultural, technological forms, materials and discourses. It has normative outcomes and draws on normative understandings. Capitalism relies on systems of finance, taxation, state economic policies of different kinds (from money supply to industrial investment), shareholders, technologies, workers and consumers, and so on. This complex of interwoven elements makes the task of understanding one among them, work, pretty hard.

'Capitalism' cannot be entirely explained or understood in the same way as made sense 10, 20, 30 or 150 years ago. It is mutable, it has echoes, and it takes forms that are familiar but distinctive in different times and places. It is affected by shifts in other social, political, technological, cultural, and economic phenomena. The theories developed by J.K. Gibson-Graham in *The end of capitalism (as we knew it)* and *A postcapitalist politics*[14] changed my ideas about how to think about capitalism. I had long ago absorbed the idea that economies were not given, but made. Human decisions, what technologies make possible, ideological preferences, legal frameworks and others all contributed to what economic activity might be, and to the socio-economic structures of capitalism. Gibson-Graham made this idea big and bold by doing the quintessentially feminist work of noticing the subtleties and invisibilities in grand accounts of capitalism. They treated capitalism as a 'regulatory fiction'[15] that erases differences through its domination, its apparent truth and reality. Capitalism seems hegemonic; it dominates all talk and understanding about economic activity.

Other economic activity seems to take place always in relation to the big structure that is capitalism, and matters only for its relationship to capitalism. In this view, the domestic sphere matters because here is where capitalism's workers are reproduced; informal economic activity is marginal to the important business of profit-making. Capitalism dominates the imagination of those who support it, and those who dislike it. Its masterfulness is seen when it appears to be heroic (as when economic growth will pull a country out of poverty), as a pinnacle of social evolution that will mark an end to scarcity and the provision of plenty, as a machine or logic that cannot be stopped. Gibson-Graham challenges this story of dominance, which they call 'capitalocentric'. They say that there are all kinds of non-capitalist economic relations in existence right now (some, like slavery, are dreadful; others, like independent commodity production, may offer a better kind of life). Non-capitalist economic relations persist, and they will not disappear in the fantasy-future of 'progress' towards 'development'. They do not merely make capitalist relations possible, but matter in their own right for how they make the world.

The results of refusing to accept the assumption that capitalism is the only game in town is, for Gibson-Graham, that we get to see how capitalism is in 'a zone of cohabitation among multiple economic forms',[16] that is, how it depends on other economic forms instead of being the container for all other forms. This has some big implications. For example, in the capitalocentric frame coffee growers with small farms, who own the means of production (tools and machines), who distribute their surplus labour and who buy and sell commodities, are capitalists, just like oil companies are capitalist.[17] Describing both as capitalist removes the important differences between these situations, differences that matter to the lives and livelihoods of small commodity producers selling global commodities. Noticing differences makes a new kind of politics possible, because new points of intervention are possible. Agents of capitalism, like big, global corporations, stop seeming like juggernauts and become entities that are deliberately constituted, that have conditions for their existence and unpredictable effects. Capitalism seems like a power formation that infects diverse places through its agent, globalisation. A standard story about globalisation is that it brings more parts of the world into the world of commodities, by creating consumer markets and by expanding the proletariat. The movements of labour are not only movements of labour-as-commodity, but also movements of people, of cultures, of families. Non-economic relations are everywhere, if only we would look.[18] Noticing economic and social diversity is a means of decontaminating this experience of infection.

The capacity to look for and see more than capitalism is at the heart of the possibility for imagining alternatives – a postcapitalist politics. Gibson-Graham have a pragmatic politics. It doesn't rely on revolutionaries or a detailed, costed fully formed plan to address that dull, dull refrain that 'There Is No Alternative'. Instead it multiplies points and forms of intervention. Ethical transformations of people happen when they do different things, and when they see that they are doing something different. The Alliance in Mumbai, for example, is an initiative that makes it possible for people living in slums to save some money.[19] These kinds of ethical self-transformation through micropolitics cannot be dismissed as trivial localism. They are important precisely because they are small-scale and ethical practice is embodied within them. They force non-humans into view, make non-humans part of the ethical questions that need asking,[20] which in turn makes the specificity of the human clearer and more distinct from the assumptions of unitary western philosophies, including those lying behind capitalocentrism. No (tacitly universal) rational actor, no autonomous human, no 'nature' on which 'culture' goes to work. As forms of economic life multiply, so too do the different kinds of entities whose continued invisibility has allowed tacitly privileged white, western male agents to seem to matter most. For Dipesh Chakrabarty,[21] decentring capitalism as *the* explanatory framework for human life is necessary to understand climate crisis. Climate crisis forces recognition of how lifeforms are connected to each other.

Capitalocentrism dominates social science understandings of work. But far from being a monolith, the capitalist landscape is disordered. Recognising existing and supporting new forms of alternative economic activism to reclaim the economy and retheorise capitalism is worth doing. Living ethics, ethics that are embodied, is the way that principles are brought into action, that is, into the world. Economic forces are contingent outcomes of ethical decisions. By whom? With what kinds of reasoning? What other ways could they be thought about? This brings me to the second big concept: ethics.

What's wrong with ethics?

Perhaps this is an age of ethics, because questions about ethics are everywhere, though it's not clear if this proliferation contributes to better lives. Rights and justice often seem to be the key principles, generating imperatives as to how to act. These are ideas with their origins in Kant, although it is US-dominated, neo-Kantian political philosophy (for example, Rawls and his interlocutors) that contributed most to the principles of ethical justice that have been sedimented into laws, regulations, guidance documents, protocols and similar. Made with the best of intentions, such documents may nonetheless have unintended effects, because regulations are always partial, and don't notice what they exclude. And they risk outsourcing ethical thinking to the documents that comprise them and the committees that write them. Technologies of control are not necessarily ethical commitments.

Rights and justice theories make universalising claims, even in the most cosmopolitan versions of ethics, which try to recognise cultural differences and reconcile that with ideas of generalised global equality and global human rights.[22] These forms of ethical thinking assume that individual moral agency is based on autonomy and rationality, and don't think about the limits to individual agency, to autonomy or rationality. On one level, it's hard in a globalised world to be against a global ethics of institutionalised responsibility. Certainly, neither ethics nor justice can follow national boundaries. But on another level, ideas such as those of human rights are abstractions that conceal the tensions in ethics between the demand for protection and the demand for freedom, and don't give much clue about the concrete modes of existence of those to whom they are applied or denied. Sharon Bolton, whose work on dignity at work will be discussed in Chapter Four, presents this conundrum clearly:

> In selling one's labour, does one also relinquish
> autonomy, freedom, equality and, often, well-being
> – the very ingredients of life that have been most
> commonly associated with human dignity? Or, is
> the case that paid work can provide the means for all
> these core elements of a quality life to be realised?[23]

Could it be that ethical thinking that is less abstract and has some
awareness of just how different people's conditions of existence
can be would be useful?

Abstract ideas about rights and justice are seductive. They seem
to make for a clear politics because they have a great propensity
to seem to be universal. But this is also their limitation: by
universalising they reject differences that might be important.
Differences might be social differences between individuals, or
they might be the harder, but more important differences of
experience: a 'concrete other', not just a generalised other.[24]
So the justice ethics that lies behind the decent work agenda
developed by the ILO (International Labour Organization, an
important UN agency with a remit to improve labour standards)
draws on mission statements and position papers can't do more
than hint at concrete differences that matter. The shorthand of
'rights' and 'justice' deny ambiguities.

The way justice ethics makes assumptions about universal
principles, rationality and objectivity combine to make ethics
an issue of individual accountability. Seem familiar? I think that
there is a remarkable similarity here between the economist's
vision of autonomous actors and that of the justice ethicists.
That ethical questions are bound up with economic ones
is fundamental *both* to how economic activity works and to
commentary on economic activity. This is seen in assertions
that markets produce desirable allocations of scarce resources –
an ethical claim if ever there was one – and, quite differently,
in the extensive and telling critique of the destructive effects
of markets on nature and on human life. The rational figure of
'economic man', disembodied and disinterested, is good friends
with the distant rational ethical observer, able to follow the
deskbound thought experiments of the utilitarian or Kantian
ethical philosopher. There is no scope here for messy life, for

feeling, for connection, for finding ethical conundrums or singular exceptions to rules and regulations. Ethicists love their thought experiments. Such desiccated games, though, don't appreciate the material, sensory and emotional complexities of everyday lives.

Open to care

The feminist argument to counter justice ethics' assumption of rational, autonomous action is to stress an ethics of care as well as an ethics of justice. Care ethics has a starting point that doesn't privilege individuals and rationality and nor does it focus on universals. This ethics speaks of connection, trust, relationships and mutual dependence, and recognises how emotion matters in judgement. It has some resonance for me, especially the ideas of interconnection and relationality. In Chapters Three and Six, I'll say more and I'll also develop a point I make in passing here, that 'care' is a contentious and complex idea that seems to be unarguably good, until I think about the power and tensions and obligations that go along with caring and being cared about. Still, because care ethics doesn't foreground a list of ethical principles, but emphasises forms of situated ethics that require reflection and engagement, it's good enough for me. It also has a benefit of inviting in non-human others too, as part of the landscape of care, work and living.[25] Where there is a humanist subject, as in most assumptions about what's wrong with work, justice is for humans only. What would an ethics of work that isn't attached to modernity's dualisms (of nature/culture) look like? Care invites me to pay attention to non-humans, to other living beings and the environments in which they live. An ethics that values the non-human alongside the human, a politics that asks for attention and care to be placed on 'nature' and nature objects results from this, following a timescale that is not rushing to find the next thing but recognises slow violence[26] and slow healing.

Like justice, care has a pragmatic value, as it calls out for particular actions and responses. Thinking with the ethics of justice gives inspiration to the idea of decent work; thinking with care gives inspiration to what work does in the world, how it affects other beings, how it damages and repairs. It makes possible a view of ethics as unfolding, as constantly displacing, and so forcing its way into consideration. Instead of the must/must not statements of moral thinking, I try to take seriously Isabelle Stengers' question of 'Who am I to say to the other, "You must" or, "You must not"?'[27] There are no recipes for cures here, quick marches from the concept of justice to a practical plan of action. Instead, there could be continuing debates that draw pragmatically on information, risks, benefits and that think about individual capacities and freedoms and self-formations, not universal ideas.

But what about Lars?

I met Lars Henriksson at an event on trade unions and green work. He's Swedish, a trade unionist, an author, an environmentalist and, for 40 years, a car assembly worker. The contradictions are writ large. Cars pollute; environmental catastrophe looms. But he wants a better world, one where his colleagues are well-treated and environmental damage is reversed. Justice and care together. How can I make sense of Lars in a way that is fair? Books and books have been written about debating the merits and problems of ideas of justice and care, and I could add to that. But Didier Fassin makes me cautious about trying. In his studies of policing in France and of global humanitarian organisations[28] he tried to apply 'ethics of justice' or 'ethics of care' to make sense of the situations that he observed. But he didn't really find *differences* when using these concepts. For example, sentiment – an effect of *care* – is important to seeing *justice* in an outcome. Sentiment is a source of conviction and feeling of responsibility. For Fassin, the ethical significance of political stances depends on history, social and cultural position (who is powerful, who is powerless). This affects the convictions people hold, their sense of responsibility, feelings. He doesn't want just to say that ethical position-taking is only *relative* to social positions. That's the kind of reasoning that makes sociology seem to be the ultimate 'science': tell me your social position and I'll tell you what you believe. What arrogance. And it doesn't help me understand Lars.

Fassin's recommendation is to attend to situations, to develop a sociology of ethics instead of a theory of ethics. He suggests three steps to doing this. First, show context. This means contextualising the interpretation of ethics, perhaps by asking when something is considered a moral or ethical issue, asking 'How is this framed as a problem?', and only then thinking about what the ethical questions raised are. Second, ask why people take the ethical stances they take. Rather than dismissing other people's ethical reasoning when it doesn't match your own, work to differentiate ethics as they are felt and understood by others. This means looking into the moral climates in which individuals live, their 'moral economies'. Third, recognise individual subjectivity. Looking at the 'moral economy' risks overstating the power of institutions, but people behave differently within the same professional and moral community. Why? With whom do they imagine they share humanity? Who is excluded? Individuals matter but they aren't the sovereignly rational basis of ethical activity.

Fassin describes this strategy as thinking about ethical issues in relation to the 'worthless rock' around them, instead of extracting and polishing them like gemstones. I am taken with this idea of thinking about ethical issues not as a discrete entity, but as something to be studied along with the rest of life. That is, to see ethics not as an abstract issue that can be extracted from everyday life, through philosophical thought experimentation, but as an impure part of human life, entwined in particular with politics of everyday life. I find the 'worthless rock' position to be useful for recognising the complexity and contingency of work, instead of trying to fit a typology of good and bad work against which everything is measurable. It asks for attention to be paid to everyday (power-filled) contexts wherein ethical issues are enacted alongside other things, where ordinary days at work involve judgement, thinking about how something emerges as having ethical dimensions, and its various mutations and formations in institutional contexts and individual reasoning. Typologies of good and bad work provide a moral economy of work, and construct a moral order; Fassin encourages the question of how different kinds of individuals encounter that moral order, position themselves by it and are positioned by it. What might this kind of approach mean for Lars?

Lars is fairly unusual in setting the problem of the environment in relation, not opposition, to the problem of (decent) work.[29] Is Lars a fool to false consciousness? A traitor to his colleagues who don't want to lose their solid jobs to some hippy ideas about greening? A capitalist cop-out who wants jobs no matter what the environmental effects are? No, let's work on a less insulting story that recognises Lars as a thinking, feeling person. Maybe Lars has an ethics that is derived from the practice of life, not from the philosopher's principles. Having an ethical concern is a structure of feeling, a relational response in an individualised world. The feelings of possibility are important. The ethical concerns are framed within specific contexts – Sweden, the car industry, Lars' family life, his union colleagues – and this affects how he asks ethical questions and what kinds of conversations he is part of, as he makes his arguments and takes his stances. Wolfgang Streeck[30] has said that capitalist crises and the feeling of end times has generated cynicism, and cynicism inhibits action and thought: it's impossible to fight against macro structures and distant power, and anything less isn't enough. But here is Lars, ignoring cynical responses and writing and campaigning. He works with the local and the small scale (knowing that this is connected to other scales), and the everyday. He thinks about ethical issues not through rules, but as made through ordinary practices. He has made possible different kinds of politics. Ethics is an active, if not stable, mediator in his life, and values have conceptual and material forms, specific to sensual and personal experiences, and are tacit.

So when I'm talking about ethics, I'm talking about how care redresses and compliments ideas of justice and injustice as it weaves work and feeling in its world-making. I'm talking about how the context in which something becomes an ethical issue affects how it is thought about and what it does. Those ethical issues when studying work are often the ethics of how other humans are treated. The intrusion of Gaia, though, forces non-humans, 'nature' and the environment into the ethics context. Working out how to care – for the human and non-human – means thinking about and working on the damages that emerge from environmental change.

After solutionism

Technology commentator Evgeny Morozov[31] describes 'solutionism' as the belief that technological solutions can be found for the whole range of 'global problems', regardless of whether the problem is real or the solution is desirable. Solutionism is the promise of eternal amelioration, a moral claim that technology, specifically of the kind developed in Silicon Valley, can apply its unique skill set and unquestionable values of efficiency, transparency and certitude, to providing 'optimised' solutions to social problems. Like Morozov, I am uncomfortable when I hear about solutions that seem to twist the problem which they are supposed to sort.

Big abstractions − ideology, capitalism, neoliberalism − that are always there, always dominant, get too easily understood as all-powerful monsters. And that makes them seem like worthy foe. That position is alluring, of course, far more so than the constant refrain you will hear from me of 'it's complicated'. But big abstractions flatten experience, assume consistency, and so deny specificities. The danger is that narrow understandings produce simplified solutions. And 'simple' is appealing, always. But it doesn't seem to be enough. You can't theorise the difficulties away. Nor can you can wish them away. But when they are still there, what is to be done?

'What's wrong with work?' is a commonly asked question with no obvious set of solutions. I would like work to be better, but what 'better' means − and indeed what 'work' means − is not that straightforward. This book synthesises current research on work in order to think through possible ways of asking and answering my three questions to get to a better understanding about work in the present. How can you find a solution when you don't know what the problem is? I will ask why questions come to be framed in the way they do, and what effect those framings have, as a way to slow down the quick ride to easy answers. As a way to find a path through, I spend some time exploring current work in this time of crisis and catastrophe. In Part One of the book, I set out a story about what contemporary work is like, what is and is not included when scholars talk about work, and discuss how things might be done differently to understand the ethical and political implications of work now. In Part Two, I take the three knotty problems that matter now: informal work, information technology work (IT) and green work as being particularly important to catastrophic times, looking at what this work does in the world and then the ethical and political questions it raises.

TWO

Work as production

Introduction

How a problem is framed and how questions about it are asked is important. Different kinds of possibilities emerge from different framings of the question. Anyone who can say what matters and what doesn't matter, and have people listen, is powerful. Putting established modes of thought and ways of describing problems under scrutiny is a way to encourage democratic conversations and different kinds of insight. Well-established modes of thinking provide important insights, and have been especially useful in understanding the effects on workers of how work is organised, both by creating strong political and ethical statements about the ways work is alienating, and by building models of 'good' and 'bad work' – both of which I discuss here. But the former doesn't do much towards understanding interconnections of work, or what work does in the world; and the latter offers apparently 'neutral tools' for the assessment of work. In the spirit of the assemblage thinking described in Chapter One, I want to open those black boxes using my feminist multi-tool, with its blades for paring out inequality, with care, caution, humility and tentativeness.

When factory work (production) is seen as the starting point, comparison point and emblematic form of work, then research, ethics and political campaigning take a particular form. That generates other omissions. Linear stories about how industrialisation originated in Europe and extended to 'peripheral' places are particular and partial, and such story telling makes invisible the historical and contemporary power of colonialism and political dominance. I consider the dominance of the factory for conceptualising work alongside the dominance of European industrialisation for conceptualising economic development because they are interconnected in many ways, including being caught together in intellectual work. That helps to see how other kinds of work exist in relation to industrial production, and to counterbalance the assumed centrality of the west. It might look like I have refused to take my own advice from Chapter One about paying attention to capitalocentric thinking. But my aim is the reverse. This chapter shows what happens when capitalocentric ideas dominate, and shows some of the absences, exclusions and partialities it makes.

Industrialisation (warning: linear narrative ahead)

The concepts scholars think with are both revealing and obfuscating. They legitimise some thoughts and delegitimise others. Critical discussions in the 19th century about the effects of industrialisation, and then again in the 20th century about the effects of scientific management and the development of production lines, are the heart of much insight into the study of work by sociologists. These critiques, developing from the problematic of Question 1 (How is work organised?), and the concepts that have been developed as a result of that framing, have generated deep understandings of the burdens and pains of (paid) work. But in avoiding the other questions, they provide only a partial understanding.

The most influential critical analysis emerged from Marx and Marxist ideas. These were developed through studying industrialised capitalism in 19th-century Europe, especially Britain. The common story goes: industrial capitalism, marked by desire for profit, private ownership, a factory system, a complicated division of labour and the routinisation of work, relied on a massive growth in the numbers of wage labourers, as well as transport infrastructures, urbanisation, mechanisation of production processes and so on, as well as new economic ideas. The new workplaces of industrial capitalism were mills, factories and coalmines, and they relied on wage labour: on men, women and children who sold their labour power in return for pay. Working bodies were controlled through disciplining mechanisms like clocks, explicit rules enforced by managers, and the rush and power of the machines themselves, so significant to industrialisation.

Marx's insights are immanent to the world. They have commented on it and shaped it. This is especially clear in relation to the development of social classes. In Marxist analysis, the key social division is between the bourgeoisie who own the means of production and the proletariat class who sell labour power. This is a powerful legacy that has generated a politics of work based in distinct class interests and that is the basis of many movements aiming to improve working conditions, for example, informing the activities of trade unions and political parties focused on workers' rights. Further, Marx's writings on alienation offer important insights into factory production. By selling wage labour in a system that subordinates creation to profit, workers cannot recognise themselves in what they make; they are alienated. The very fact of living in capitalism creates alienation: alienation from nature, from fellow humans, from the act of producing and from the products of their work. It can't be helped; it's part of the objective conditions of capitalist life, and it makes for misery.

Factory work

The common story about factory work has a 20th-century manifestation too. Scientific management emerging from the workplace observations of Frederick Taylor, combined with the rationalising desires of Lillian and Frank Gilbreth, respectively, a psychologist and a time and motion expert (famous as the inspiration for the original *Cheaper by the Dozen*) and with the insights of a host of other American experts, was welcomed by manufacturing companies. It seemed to promise a compliant workforce, a smooth production process, and a regulatory structure that enabled profit making, emblematised in the Fordist production line that emerged in the early 20th century. Here was a heightened, extended, measured and apparently efficient division of labour created by applying technorational theories to human 'inputs'. New machines both reflected and sharpened the separation of mental and manual labour, so much so that other work was re-organised in the style of factory work. The combination of typewriters and increasing numbers of women able to use them changed clerical work, for example. Related transformations such as the emergence of human resource management and psychological understandings of workplace behaviours described by Illouz[1] as the coming of 'emotional capitalism' were part of new modes of workplace control based on new forms of management knowledge. In the words of Boltanski and Chiapello,[2] this was a 'new spirit of capitalism', marked by bureaucratic management.

Sociological insights into the effects and implications of Taylorist production for workers came in the 1960s. This is the time when the discipline of sociology expanded, and was even a bit cool. The 'sociology of industrial societies', a subdiscipline where discussions about work took place, studied manufacturing to explore issues of status and belonging for male workers such as the car workers in Luton studied by Goldthorpe et al.[3] Alienation was a buzzword, developed by Marxist writers such as Herbert Marcuse[4] to make sense not only of work, but of the rest of life, and most insightfully for studies of work, by Robert Blauner in the compellingly titled *Alienation and freedom*.[5] Alienation for Blauner is not an absolute objective state (as for Marx), but varies according to four factors: the degree of control over work, the sense of purpose of work, the degree of social integration with colleagues and the degree of involvement with work. Blauner's typology was intended to make it easy to compare work of different kinds.

Critical Marxist accounts of the production line take Braverman's *Labour and monopoly capital: The degradation of work in the twentieth century*[6] as the lodestar. This, and the factory ethnographies it inspired[7] – were essential to a set of concepts for studying work known as labour process theory (LPT). This tradition has been effective in generating analyses with resonance for understanding the damages of work. It prioritises three problems with wage labour: that wage labour brings exploitation as the worker receives less than the value their work adds (they are alienated in Marx's sense of that concept);

that workers cede control of their bodies for the duration of work; and that managerial control over workers' bodies is achieved by degrading work processes to make them require less skill. Workers are bored, their tacit knowledges unrecognised and unrewarded, their potential and autonomy denied. The politics of work that emerge from this focus on the wage labourer's conditions of employment and their capacity to resist management control. There is no escape from being alienated at work. Other ways of studying and commenting on the ethics of work that emerged in the 1960s share ideas about political consensus and the centrality of class identity, and make similarly capitalocentric assumptions. Drawing on Blauner's ideas that alienation is not the same everywhere, some made pragmatic arguments about making work better.

The quality of working life

Quality of working life (QWL) research emerged in the US, UK and Scandinavia in the 1960s to understand the problems of factory work. It aimed to emancipate workers through action at the level of the firm/organisation. As in the case of labour process theories, it reflects the concerns of its times. It drew on social psychology to address two problems of the day. The first problem was the rather paternalistic concern about how people were recruited to support extremist political parties because they were alienated by their work. Memories of European fascism and contemporary fear of communism mattered. Also in the air of the 1960s, exploding in the spirit of 1968, was a new politics of human life, a politics of subjectivity and identity beyond social class.[8] QWL programmes offered a kind of humane capitalism by working on designing jobs that might not be completely dreadful to do. Designing better jobs meant thinking about what made good work. The 1960s list (with brief explanation) included:

- compensation (pay and benefits);
- safe and healthy (avoids damage to bodies and minds);
- develops human capacity (skill development, involved in decisions);

- growth and security (employability, personal development);
- social integration (organisational climate);
- constitutionalism (employee rights and representation);
- total life (work–life balance);
- social relevance (social responsibility in organisation).

Two 'good' attributes to bring the list into line with 21st-century ideas about what people want from life are individual proactivity, where a worker can show initiative in a supportive context, and flexible work that benefits the worker, rather than just the organisation.[9] These ideas reflect the idea that 'good' work is not only a question of pay and skill, but also of secure work that feels meaningful, with good colleagues.[10] Like Marilyn Strathern, though, I suspect bullet points 'allow no growth…create no knowledge'[11] because they carry no meaning. Or rather, the meaning they carry is the same kind of meaning as a shopping list. There is no space for contradiction or compensation, or complexity. What on earth do these attributes actually feel like in work? On the one hand, they're impossible to disagree with, but on the other hand, that's because it's not clear what they involve, or how they can be achieved. It's complete but it's not coherent.

QWL faded away in part because alternative management strategies emerged. Kaizen movements that organise work to encourage worker commitment have similarities, but 'lean production' ideas showed little interest in the conditions under which employees worked (as 'lean' is translated as 'cheap'); 'human resource management' went for quick fixes like statements about not tolerating bullying – far easier and cheaper than getting rid of bullies. QWL left some important insights. One is that how managers and technicians design jobs is important to how they are experienced. Another is that the firm is one point where action to improve work can be taken. As firms are full of contestation and outcomes are not given or fixed,[12] structures of ownership and the activities of different social groups, including corporate managers, financiers, shareholders, suppliers and labour, combine differently. Clearly, factory work captured the imagination of sociologists of work as they tried to make sense of the effects of how this work was organised on those who did it. It's right to have concepts to understand factory work, which remains a significant global employer. In both Marxist and non-Marxist theories for thinking about what's wrong with work, social class is key. That bothers me.

Exclusions of gender and race 'on the shopfloor'

Of the many, many ethnographic studies of factory work, I've picked one to show how easy it is for researchers to obscure important features of working lives. Donald Roy's 'Banana time'[13] has become a classic study for insights into play and boredom in factory work. It discusses the games that four machine operatives (George, Ike, Sammy and Donald himself) make up to help time pass as they do incredibly repetitive jobs. In reading Roy's paper, it's easy to miss that there's another person in the room with them, referred to only twice. Once as 'a female employee who performed sundry scissors operation of a more intricate nature on raincoat parts ... [in] a cell within a cell'[14] and a second time as Baby, one of two black women who held that job during Roy's research. Roy's gang warn any black male workers who come to pick up the work they've done to 'Stay away from Baby! She's Henry's girl.'[15] Baby's own thoughts on her gendered and racialised sexualisation are not recorded, nor does she ever get to join in the games. Black women's factory work is almost invisible to Roy. That means that the ideas that emerge from his analysis, and others like it, are taken as a general statement about factory work, not a specific statement about being a male, white, American, unionised factory worker, with a male, American boss. Play at work for Roy is about games between men. Play at work to me looks like a way to create outsiders. Sexual harassment in factories hasn't disappeared[16] and maybe Baby would now want to say #metoo.

Race is absolutely part of how work and employment are organised.[17] It is part of labour market segregation that means black women in the US at the time of Roy's study were more likely to be domestic or service workers, but also that when employed in the same place as Ike, George et al, gender and racial job stereotyping meant that they did not do the same work.

Specifics of locale affect the interplay of gender, race, labour and citizenship.[18] And, given anti-discrimination legislation and the appearance of a more equal society, job segregation in the US has changed considerably. While formal discrimination may be outlawed, practices of exclusion persist. But even in organisations that decry racism and deny structural racism, white managers persist in finding that their black employees simply 'don't quite fit' in to the culture.[19]

There has been lots of research since that counters these kinds of absences, silences and denials that made Baby invisible. But they always have to make a case for themselves against assumed norms: the ways of studying work are already set by concepts and ideas established from the norms of male factory work. This is why the metaphors for work that persist are the factory floor and the production line, the shopfloor and the coalface. They are not bedsides or desks. To my mind, the gendering and racialisation of work is not an 'add on' feature. When current discussions of work still expect to draw on concepts and ideas developed in factory settings during the first and second 'spirits of capitalism', and are policed according to whether they do that, those concepts get extended into settings that they don't suit. The effect is of a narrow and narrowing understanding of what work is like that theorises from a position that doesn't recognise specificity – the specificity of the job being talked about and its location in time and space, and the specificity of the kind of people who hold that job. One route to rethinking these concepts is to go back to the starting assumptions about the importance of industrialisation, and see if a different story can be told.

Start again: empire, colonialism, slavery

The simple tale of 19th-century industrialisation in Britain, familiar from school textbooks, relies on a partial account of industrial society and capitalism – 'First Europe, then elsewhere' theories,[20] that position Europe as the model for development to which other places might aspire. Tell the story differently and other implications for what work then and now is like blossom forth. All those cotton mills of northern England that seemed to be the core of industrialisation relied on imports of raw cotton, and to pretend otherwise is 'seriously to distort history'.[21] In the early 19th century, English cotton products were in competition with fashionable and cheap Indian cottons (social change and consumer culture matters to how work is organised). Indian cottons were made in small-scale family and community units, informally organised. Informal organisation, reshaped but recognisable, was maintained through the colonial era, enabling British-based textile industries to benefit from cheap labour.[22] The development of plantation cotton production in the Americas led to a new source of raw cotton, and a change to the global shape of production and consumption. Conquest, colonialism and the reshaping of the world that emerged through slavery and indentured agricultural work was essential to the emergence of industrialisation in Europe.

Of course, global trade in luxuries like silk, spices and coffee has a long, long history. Historians studying the Silk Road have shown how people, ideas and cultures migrated with trade goods between China and central Asia.[23] The desire for luxury is one of the ways consumption is important to trade and so to work. There have been intensive and extensive debates among economic historians as to how best to understand the relationship between trade, war and conquest, the technological changes of industrialised production, and the social relations between people and places. World systems theory, trying to find explanation for persistently uneven economic development, argues that global capitalism – which means a deeper, more sustained importance of market exchange than global trade – emerged in the 17th century as a result of colonial and imperialist expansion strategies of Europe from the 16th and 17th centuries.[24] Political dominance through exploration, war and conquest is an outcome of the desire of capital to expand its reach and its profit-making power. 'Global' capitalism involves 'core' countries dominating peripheral regions, extracting their natural resources to support industrial production.

So global trade, production and consumption were entwined with politics and domination, reliant on dualist hierarchies that associated whiteness with rationality and reason, and darker skin with untamed and uncivilised nature. Colonialism is legitimated through such claims, as is slavery. The history of industrialisation is inseparable from this history of colonialism and slavery, with the Atlantic triangle of trade in cotton, sugar and people a most venomous part of this. Historians have debated how to understand the relationship between capitalism and slavery since Eric Williams[25] argued for the interdependence of slavery and capitalist competition. Both the economies of scale of plantation production and the financial value of slave ownership in the Americas contributed to industrialisation in Europe. This history is being examined now for the light it sheds on persistent, contemporary racial inequalities in the US. I follow Laura Pulido[26] in thinking that race is not contained by or reducible to capitalism, but race differences are crucial to accumulating profit and power. Both land and labour, means through which value is acquired (profit, power) are suffused with racial differences, through the legacy of colonial land appropriation and the long sting in slavery's tail. And as colonialism and slavery were important to industrialisation, they are still important to its present.

Exploration and conquest transformed natural environments, through accidentally imported diseases and deliberately planted crops and animals, places 'discovered' by European explorers changed.[27] Land was appropriated from indigenous people; land values and land expansion contributed to the economic effects of plantations. Colonised places had desirable natural resources, such as fertile land for growing food for export, precious metals and mineral resources and other raw materials. New kinds of agriculture and new kinds of care came to be needed. The rhythms of work on land and agricultural work are different to those in the factory, where clock-time dominates seasonal time. Human history is inescapably entwined with natural history. Histories have present effects. When tourist brochures now offer unsullied nature and self-effacing service in luxury Caribbean hotels, for example, they suppress histories of land theft, forced removal, coercion and slavery.

Slavery as work

What would happen to understandings of work, however, if they took slavery, coerced labour and indentured labour seriously as being as much at the heart of industrialisation processes as wage labour? The making of commodified human life into a resource for production, justified by false racial hierarchies, and by claims about the civilising virtues of trade and manufacturing, was (and is) an uglier exploitation of human labour than the wage labour systems in factories and mills. At the least it means that a politics of class needs also to be a politics of race that takes seriously the intersection of racialised hierarchies with economic and political inequalities that were and are central to capitalism. Justice ethics privileges freedom and autonomy, the free universal subject, but slavery makes it clear that this is only freedom for some. Making sense of this needs a subtle understanding of how ethical principles emerge in specific times and spaces.

While now wage labour dominates and so the politics of wage labour may seem more obviously important, slavery did not disappear in the 19th century with abolition legislation. It is still present today, alongside other deeply unpleasant ways of organising work such as indentured labour, that can only persist if people are happy to accept that hierarchies between kinds of people are valid; it marks a failure of enlightenment and liberal values of 'justice' that Human Rights declarations and Decent Work agendas have not had the power to counter. Indeed, forced labour is still the standard management practice for cotton producers in Uzbekistan, supported and enabled by the national government.[28]

The 2017 Global Slavery Index estimates 40 million people in slavery of different forms. Its estimates are conservative, because slavery is often hidden: 16 million slaves work in the private sector, half of whom are in debt bondage; nearly 4 million are in forced commercial sex work, and just over 4 million in state-enforced labour; 15 million are in forced marriage, and so doing domestic work; 71 per cent of all enslaved people are women or girls. Chattel slavery, where people are born, captured or sold into slavery; debt bondage, where people are pledged against loans that never get paid off; and false contract slavery, where people think they are signing up to contracted work but are the powerless, are all present. If contemporary slavery is seen as exceptional, the acts of a few bad criminals, then it is easy to legitimate seeing it as *outside* of discussions of contemporary work. The more work is seen as paid wage labour, the more invisible unfree labour is, the more exceptional it is. Bringing unfree work into discussions with other kinds of work brings to the fore the politics of human bodies as commodities. Unfree labour is mixed into supply chains. It is in plain sight in shrimp farming in Sundarbans bay, for example, which uses forced child labour and which destroys mangroves that protect the area from flooding.[29] Those knots are tightly wound. Slavery and colonialism have had lasting effects on coloniser and colonised places. The inequalities of the present are knotted to those of the past. They are not natural. They are even re-made in the present through global governance structures (like The World Bank – more on that in Chapter Five).

Global production and global inequalities

The long reach of colonial exploitation matters in order to understand racialised differences in the kinds of work people do, and in how they are treated at work, in ways that I don't think can be reduced to a class position that expresses a relationship to waged work in factories. Sticking with the capitalocentric arguments for now helps to see contemporary global interconnections of work. Changes to how work is organised, to occupations, to how firms operate, to the global division of labour, and to transnational and financialised trade mark the present as very different from the 19th century, and it looks pretty obvious that capitalist operations don't take the same form that they did in the era of scientific management. The interconnections and disjunctures of economic activity in the present are affected by the past. How can I make sense of this knot? Most tools are broad-brush, capitalocentric concepts that characterise epochs/periods. They illuminate, but they also cast shadows.

It's a common strategy to characterise an epoch by adding a qualifier to 'capitalism' to highlight a feature that seems especially appropriate to describing the current moment. Cognitive capitalism,[30] for example, considers now as a time where the 'knowledge economy' dominates, whereby markets harness public opinion and attention, and production harnesses consumer feedback through prosumption and just-in-time production.

It might explain constant transmission of information by and about consumers but it doesn't touch the economy of favours and exchanges in Moscow.[31] In focusing in on some elements of contemporary life, capitalism qualifiers leave other elements blurry. They make invisible the persistence of old or different patterns within and alongside shiny new phenomena.

Adequate concepts for a 'global' world

A far more popular concept, globalisation is the easy shorthand for a world that is marked by connections, networks and interdependencies between distant and nearby places. Since the 1990s, globalisation has been a go-to concept for thinking about the interconnections between places, initially as a rather all-consuming idea that heralded the flattening of differences. The headline argument is that economic, political and cultural processes are transnational: trade, capital, finance and the organisation of production and consumption are interlinked, and increasingly so. Predatory capitalism, looking for new inputs and new markets, drives globalisation, and IT makes it possible.

Globalisation is a brittle concept, though, and shatters when it is used to do much explanatory work. Especially worrisome are those theories that see globalisation as an inevitable evolution from a less to a more connected world, running along rails already set out; or as a universalising and homogenising process whereby capital is made mobile in the interests of multinational corporations and corporate elites. Indeed, as researchers found more sophisticated ways to recognise the contingency of globalisation and the solid, ongoing presence of local specificities, a different all-consuming concept, neoliberalism, emerged to supplant globalisation.[32] I think of globalisation as a concept that draws attention to how the practices of connection and dependency are made through the actions of agents, exchanges, institutions, networks and regulations, emerging from the history of global trade and conflict. Globalisation is a practice or tendency, not a done deal: there are no linear narratives or simple causations here, and there are persistent localising tendencies.[33]

As it encourages generalisations, 'globalisation' doesn't force attention to what geographers call 'uneven development' or 'variegated capitalism',[34] or to what the world systems guys call 'core' and 'periphery'. I'd like to find concepts that acknowledge the legacies of racial inequalities to 'capitalism' in the present, in recognition of how language choices are world-making and reflect understanding of inequalities. Chandra Mohanty's discussion[35] – and willingness to vary terminology – is very useful in looking for ways of characterising a connected but differentiated world. The once common distinction between first and third worlds (largely mapping onto the core/periphery distinction discussed earlier) is rarely used now because of the explicit hierarchy it contains, and because it assumes a linear path to development, although Mohanty says that it is sometimes useful to point out the legacy of colonialism. 'Less developed countries' (LDC), commonly used in global policy, implies that economic development is a single-track road to an inherently desirable destination.

Mohanty assesses common alternatives. Global North and Global South are often used, the former referring to affluent and privileged nations, and the latter to politically marginalised and economically disadvantaged nations (see also the geographically inaccurate 'west', which is set against an undifferentiated 'rest'). This is perhaps best thought of as a metaphoric rather than a geographic difference (Australia, physically south, is nonetheless 'western'/privileged). Mohanty uses this frame some of the time, but is also a fan of the metaphoric 'one-third–two-thirds' worlds' developed by Gustavo Esteva and Madhu Suri Prakash.[36] The minority world is the world of privilege, with a modern, technologically sophisticated, consumption-heavy way of life. The minority world works in formal employment. The two-thirds majority world may live in and among the minority, providing services in global cities, if not accessing the apparent benefits of global interconnections. These concepts are shorthand for the unequal race, class, nation, sex and migration status of people.

Just-in-time

Globalisation is bound up with changes to the organisation of production and consumption, with technologies and managerial strategies for making, distributing and selling goods, commonly described as post-Fordism. Fordist production was connected to scientific management, the assembly line and to research into the effects of technological change on manufacturing work. At best (for those with jobs), internal labour markets and training meant that a career within one company was possible, with workplace benefits negotiated by active trade unions. Worker retention mattered to firms because of the cost of staff turnover (recruitment and training). Post-Fordist production is quite different. It dates loosely to the economic crises of overproduction in the 1970s and seems to promise a situation where supply of consumer goods will never again exceed demand. Pumped up by more powerful IT, post-Fordist production gathers and communicates cultural information in order to be flexible in production and give choice to consumers. Information is the key commodity. Consumers' response to brands is a prime example of communicative and cultural values being stirred into production decisions. Consumer preferences can be measured by stock monitoring and now by the kinds of brokering technologies that follow shoppers around the internet with recommendations for stuff they probably don't want. Information about inventories, about demand for products and demand for work are equally desirable to create maximum profit with minimal cost. Norms for making use of labour change. Production costs are reduced by removing benefits to labour and by flexibilising so that production is 'just-in-time'.

One version of the new flexibility was flexible specialisation. This seemed to offer better work: if production was organised so as to be responsive to markets, then it might require skilled workers making use of a range of tools and technologies, able to be creative and innovative and get ahead of the game. It might need craft work, not tedious routine labour. It might involve employing people able to do a wide range of tasks. This was a slice of pie in the sky. As it turned out, the broader shift to the flexible firm created more of the other kind of flexibility: numerical flexibility, where unnecessary workers could be quickly dispensed with. Flexibilising work most often means varying contracted hours; it can also mean moving production to other places where labour is cheaper or tax breaks are better; or subcontracting another company to provide a service.

Outsourcing, 'footloose capital' and the development of extended supply chains became the new normal, encouraged by nation-states offering tax incentives, special enterprise zones, agreements to restrict labour rights, to encourage business. Economists in non-state organisations such as The World Bank are also actively promoting flexible labour markets. Changes to the financial and operational structure of corporations (brand valuation and brand equity), financialisation and the power of institutional/distant shareholders affected how companies acted. As globalisation is shadowed by colonial pasts, so are the more specific social and economic relations entailed in post-Fordist just-in-time practices. Fragmented flexibilised production draws on and reproduces global differences to extract value, cheapen labour and deregulate. The marked cost to this kind of flexibility is born by those working flexibly (see Chapter Five). That is the cost of the race to the bottom: globalised competition lowers wages; lower wages mean low quality of life.

Global production networks

With global trade, flexibilised production, IT and logistics, there is no characteristic workplace like the Fordist car factory making an entire Model T. Instead, there are extenuated supply chains, networks of economic actors connecting raw materials and finished goods. Flexible production is especially common in labour-intensive consumer goods industries such as clothing and furniture, where global production networks (GPNs) dominate (supply chains and commodity chains are other terms for this process). GPNs are 'factories without walls',[37] production is global but labour is atomised and local: poorly paid and badly treated manufacturing workers sit on assembly lines and sew, solder and screw together consumer goods. They are invisible to other parts of the network.

Offshoring and outsourcing are common ways that branded garment retailers create GPNs that maintain distance between different stages in the production of goods to be sold. Middle*men* (and these intermediaries usually are men, reflecting the wide-ranging and longstanding gendering of power at work) negotiate with multiple small sewing factories over the sewing of clothes. The factories that get subcontracted are pushed by the threat of losing the contract to doing the work more cheaply. The trade-off for keeping the contract is low wages. Using intermediaries and distant suppliers enables 'deniability', so the lead firm can keep its brand value by throwing their hands up in despair when confronted with news of exploitation in the supply chain and say 'It wasn't us, guv, we didn't know.' Garment manufacture is an easy case to consider, not least because serious incidents such as the fire at Rana Plaza, Bangladesh, in 2013, that claimed 1,134 lives, means that people are aware that brand retailers do not make their own products, but outsource to other companies. As commodity chain researchers have shown in Turkey,[38] relationships between the brand and suppliers are unequal; the big brand can walk away from a contract more readily than its small and dependent suppliers.

A subcontract of a subcontract of a subcontract is not unheard of, although organisational networked relationships are not the only kind of distanced flexibility and hands-off intervention. Labour intermediaries – perhaps employment agencies, perhaps gangmasters – provide extra workers. They coordinate information about work demand and supply. The 'cascade' of intermediaries, positioned between the ultimate producer and the direct employer of labour, although sometimes remote from either, buffer producers/lead firms from the accusations that they use forced or unfree labour.[39] Labour contractors may be de facto employers on behalf of producers. How the labour contractor behaves is therefore critical to the quality of flexible work, to whether it offers 'social upgrading'[40] through better conditions of work, gaining skills, or moving to regulated sectors or organisations. Cheap workers in vulnerable situations whose presence can be denied – or are at least hidden – from view are common, though. It's a pretty easy question to remember to ask: if it's cheap for you, who paid the price? Slave labour is used in supply chains, hidden from view by the very complicated systems of contracting and subcontracting.[41] Forced labour is no 'residual' condition of underdevelopment that will be got rid of through economic development. It is part and parcel of an unequal global production system, where the terms of inclusion into global capitalism are dreadful. This 'adverse incorporation'[42] is intrinsic to the economic system, reliant on racial and geographic inequalities between people.

Making production possible

It's easy to think about supply chains in relation to manufacture, but of course all kinds of other work are involved. Fashion and design work, marketing and advertising, the creation and maintenance of retail outlets, perhaps an online site or a supermarket or a market stall; materials extraction; machine design, production and maintenance; the shipping and logistics that transports components, finished products and waste. These kinds of work are connected but also radically different. They are ordinary, sometimes invisible, and taken for granted.

The commercial work that produces consumption – product design, branding, advertising, marketing and so on – contribute to how GPNs are made and recreated. If the 'brand offer' is cheap, fast fashion, then outsourced suppliers get squeezed. Certainly a range of work goes into creative feelings, desires and needs that contribute to and satisfy consumer urges, to organising the consumption of goods and services, and to providing other business services from patent lawyers to 'solutions engineers'. Requiring educational credentials, higher status and higher paid than the outsourced production work discussed already, some of that commercial work is nonetheless precarious. Short-term relationships and contracts, relying on networks for the next job, suggest that callous 'non-standard' employment practices of the service sector have been extended into creative labour,[43] and more recently into other formerly secure middle-class jobs. Further, service provision is also networked and entangled similarly to production networks, for example, where business-processing services are offshored,[44] or when advertising agencies set up 'local' offshoots of global agencies.

GPNs depend on IT software and hardware, internet connections, computer-aided design abilities, apps for stock checking and logistics tracking, platforms, and so many other kinds of other IT. Hidden technologies to master 'nature' such as under-sea fibre optic cables that enable high speed information exchange, taken-for-granted technologies that were once transformative (electronic points of sale [EPOS], for example), and simple transformations of work (online booking systems) are all designed and produced. The acronym 'IT' doesn't do justice to the complex practices and corporate structures of software programs and hardware, to research and development, or to understandings of information gathering and analysis. Flexible production depends on gathering and calculating data in order to plan. In the crucial field of logistics, for example, calculation practices developed in the 1960s, infrastructures were refined in the 1970s and 'the capacity for countries to participate in the physical circulation of global trade became itself a measure of development' in the 1990s.[45] GPNs work on the principle that anything that sits still doesn't make any money. Just-in-time production and distribution keeps components and finished goods moving – inventories are a sink of value, they cost money to look after and they don't create any profit. Whoever holds stock (perhaps the suppliers of large corporate buyers) finds their bottom line squeezed. So the more the lead firm works with lots of reorders that have to be met quickly, the more pressure on the supplier.[46]

Flows of information, which appear to compress time and space to re-scale the globe as much smaller, are privileged in globalisation accounts in a way that the movement of material components, finished goods and waste products are not. That movement is via container shipping and air freight, along motorways to distribution warehouses, around the warehouse and out again to a delivery van. Making those movements possible are flexible workers who still need to eat and sleep, whose children go to school and whose bad backs might get treated with painkillers. Logistics infrastructures make movement/mobility possible. This relies on work done on infrastructures, in port cities[47] and on container ships,[48] by data inputters and software technicians. Logistics is a paradigm for the present, the world rendered on one plane, the fine outcome of technorationality, the grounds for economic efficiency, optimised outcomes and for linking global and local *just in time*. While it has reverberations of the past of global trade and military dominance, including the sugar–slave–cotton triangle, it has a distinctly modern rhythm marked by both the slow and inexorable movement of container ships and the considerably faster movement of data about what is where, who wants what, and what labour it will take to make that happen. Interdependencies are not only directly historical ones, but are produced and reproduced by, for example, corporate decisions as to how to organise production – where they locate it, the tax subsidies they might get, what some kinds of technologies make possible, and so on. This means that the connections of economic activity are also connections of global inequality.

Moving on

Taking up Gibson-Graham's critique of capitalocentrism, there is a problem here in that everything is explained in relation to the coming of capitalism, defined as a single all-conquering economic system, from which political and social systems derive. I don't buy that. The history of sociology is wound up in the history of studying work, with an implicit history of ethical reasoning and moral claims. There are clear interconnections between how economy activity is thought about and how work is thought about. I have shown that the concepts initially used by sociologists studying work emerged from their analysis of industrialisation and then Fordist production and talked about how that connects to a broader knowledge of and politics of work (class politics). But that left some things out of view. When a different story is told about 19th- and 20th-century work, a story that recognises global trade and political dominance – that is, when colonial dominance is considered – the past and present start to look quite different.

It is not only unfree work that emerges into the light when looking through the lens of this broader history. The failure to consider the implications of, say, the shifting organisation of clerical work in the 20th century for the ideas about alienation and exploitation when thinking about politics, the struggle to incorporate an account of the politics of life beyond work (gender, consumption) into the politics of work, and the privileging of class inequality about all, have all contributed to a situation where a Marxist politics of work has too narrow an understanding of the politics of work. I do not argue that alienation, resistance and exploitation are not present in contemporary work; only that these concepts emerged in particular ways at a particular time, and were grounded in exclusions and absences.

THREE

Deleted labour and hidden work

Introduction

Time and again, I read the formula 'From X to Y', where X is the past and Y is the present: industrial to post-industrial; Fordist to post-Fordist; manufacturing economy to service economy. The newer version of this formula is more complex: from the first to the second to the third to (now) the fourth industrial revolution. The first was mechanisation, the second was mass production, the third is automation and the fourth is the digitalisation of life itself, including artificial intelligence (AI), robots and nanotechnology. For some, this fourth stage heralds the 'end of work',[1] a transformation of work that means humans won't have to do it. This kind of commentary is not to my taste. It assumes a straight line of progress, and it has a deliberately simplistic idea about what kinds of economic activity matter: the production of things. There is nothing outside of technorational capitalist production. In this chapter, I will disassemble these assumptions about work with my feminist multi-tool.

There is a refrain in this book that concepts create exclusions and that makes for absences in understanding. When work practices are forgotten, ignored, excluded, not seen or denied, then any account of the ethical and political issues in doing work is restricted. In the last chapter, I followed other sociologists in putting paid work in factories at the centre, following capitalocentric and western-dominated reasoning. Once industrialisation was positioned in relation to war, conquest, colonialism and slavery, it started to be easier to notice different kinds of work and to understand persistent geographic and racial inequalities. Even so, many, many loose threads were left dangling. Counterbalancing the obsession with productive work doesn't mean rejecting it, of course. But by avoiding capitalocentrism and linear stories, this chapter makes visible work that is too readily and easily deleted. Without an inclusive idea about what we talk about when we talk about work, there is no hope for understanding what's wrong with work.

Loose threads

There are some loose threads from Chapter Two around the theme of the history of industrialisation and its implicit relationship with consumption, non-production work and pre-industrial work. Industrialisation often goes hand in hand with urbanisation. Wage workers in cities have to buy food and clothes, rather than making their own. So, wage workers are consumers, and buy in the products of other work. The thread of colonialism is sewn into consumer culture and the service work it relies on. In the late 19th century, it was common for the grand department stores of the major cities in Europe to set up special displays of 'exotic' goods, often the products of colonised countries. Here is a small example of how new kinds of promotional work that brought together production and consumption were involved in creating ideas about gender, race and class. The work of colonised people was implicitly present in displays of seemingly exotic items in western department stores; promotional strategies like 'Empire Week' in Britain in 1922[2] saw white British housewives demonstrate imperial fervour and distant caring by feeling proud and kind when they bought products made in colonised places.

In the last chapter, I talked about how marketers, advertisers and shop assistants and other service workers make contemporary GPNs possible, along with manufacturing and distribution workers. These occupations were also important to industrialisation, even if the details of how to do the job have changed over time.

In addition, industrialisation relied on vast state and non-state bureaucracy. Civil servants, bureaucrats, managers and clerical workers, and so on were, and are, involved in governing (working) populations. Add in work in education and health, and other sectors which are both organised and institutionalised differently between places, and which grew in importance in the comings and goings of different elements of what could once, if no longer, be described as a welfare state. These workers are harder to understand through the lens of the class division of labour of industrial work. Service and clerical work is invisible in early theorisations of the politics of work, and so the key tension in work is imagined to be between boss and worker. There may be little class ambiguity for mill workers, but there are many hierarchies in service work that are not reducible to the question of the ownership of the means of production. Furthermore, class politics rested on gendered exclusion, as when on-the-ground campaigns about improving the working lives of shop girls went alongside resistance from labour unions to recognising women's work, as in the case of the culinary unions in the US that did not want to let waitresses in.[3] Gendered exclusions from trade unions still matter, especially in informal sectors such as garment workers in Bangladesh, who are better supported by NGO activities.[4]

Those easy tales of industrialisation mentioned in Chapter Two imply that production work done in the home – weaving and spinning, for example – was mechanised and transformed into wage labour. That's the relentless march of technologically facilitated progress towards marketisation. But the preindustrial persists in the face of this apparently inexorable capturing of life by markets. It persists not only in 'less developed' places, but also in the most thoroughly marketised societies. People still go foraging for mushrooms (even in the US), to eat and to sell to expensive restaurants, connecting the precarious vulnerabilities of those who forage with the food fetishists who want obscure and rare products.[5] Foraging is not scalable into the kinds of mega-production in supply chains talked about in Chapter Two, not least because nature ignores consumer desire. A great example of this is Henry Ford's failure to apply intensified mass production line ideas to growing rubber trees.[6] The matter of nature just would not be conquered by technorationality. Technorationality also cannot predict or conquer what matters to people, as I learned from Thom Davies'[7] study of people who live near Chernobyl who go mushrooming in contaminated zones, as they always used to. Old traditions and present desires overwhelm the threat of nuclear contamination.

Invisible and deleted work

The view from globalisation and post-Fordism brings global factory work into sight, in the form of the maquiladoras in Mexico, Foxconn in China, Rana Plaza in Bangladesh and thousands of other factory sites that are not so infamous, even if they deserve to be. That view leaves much else, including much other work in a state of 'non-existence', in Boaventura de Sousa Santos' phrase. Santos says that when an entity is disqualified and invisible it is produced into non-existence.[8] Entities that are ignorant, residual, inferior, local and non-productive are disappeared, because if they cannot be captured by the usual modes of thought, they simply cannot exist. If and when non-existent entities do bubble up, then sense must be made of them, and if they cannot, then they remain evidence of mysticised difference and of the validity of hierarchies. In the case of 'already existing diverse economies',[9] entities and practices that are incomprehensible through dominant modes of thought like capitalism, justice or technorationality cannot really matter. So work that is not work (because it is not paid, or is also a familial obligation, or because it makes something that is never exchanged),[10] that is not connected to global production, supply chains and consumption, is not explainable through hierarchical dualisms that rely on creating a totality for reasoning and understanding. So perhaps it does not exist!

Erin Hatton defines invisible work as work that is 'economically devalued'[11] through an interplay of socio-cultural, socio-legal and socio-spatial 'mechanisms' (in Hatton's terms), or processes and practices (in mine). Work is made invisible (to those not doing it) by cultural norms that don't recognise the importance of some kinds of labour, through the legal and regulatory frameworks that define what counts as work, and in the literal visibility and invisibility of places where work happens. In domestic service work, for example, the economic, the legal, the cultural and the spatial are entangled in making it invisible: here is a gendered and racialised kind of work that is done in private settings by people who are sometimes documented or undocumented migrants, who do work that is not regulated by contracts or minimum wages. Specific invisibility mechanisms operate. They devalue women's 'natural' abilities to care, for example, or put work out of sight in order to get it out of mind, or make assumptions about skill and craft that deny the complexity of work (of which, more in Chapter Four). For me, this invisibility of work, this denial of it, is a problem.

Work is invisible work when its effects are disappeared. Dirty work tends to be hidden away, done at times of the day when other people are not around. It becomes noticeable when it fails – when cleaners or rubbish collectors go on strike. As Chapter Eight will show, waste materials are made invisible by being exported, left for invisible workers elsewhere, often in the Global South, often former colonised places, to deal with. Invisible work that happens out of sight in places that seem far away is easy to ignore. This work is hidden because it is shameful to think of it. Think, for example, about how cheap clothes are made. They can only be made by invisible workers, because if real, visible workers worked in those conditions, then no one could justify buying them. It would be shameful to buy them, like buying elephant tusks or fur. Reframing the ethics and politics of work has to involve seeing this kind of invisible work in settings where it would be easy to continue to deny it: in this instance in relation to consumption as well as in relation to work.

Invisible labour is akin to deleted labour, a concept useful for showing how non-humans are involved in how work is done. The idea comes from Susan Leigh Star's argument that inequalities emerge 'as the work of negotiating, resource management, and many other processes are deleted from representations, one group's interests begin to take precedence over another's, subverting the fundamental pluralism of human interaction'.[12] Labour is deleted in order to smooth the telling of a story, or to smooth the experience of work. It makes work activities seem simpler. Science becomes a simple process of discovery, often from the mind of a Great Inventor, not a practice that is contentious, and that is dependent on there being tools and techniques available, nor a clean lab staffed by well-fed scientists. Policy-making becomes a simple process of applying an agreement, not a hard-fought negotiation. Deletion is part of how the promise of technorational governance is made, as it makes processes seem easy and inevitable. So, software technologies that appear to just emerge makes it seem like the work of coders – and their assumptions about the world – don't matter. Deleting labour contributes to the idea that some work seems to matter more than others. Surgeons cure illnesses, but care assistants clean people who are ill: both matter for the prospect of a healthy future. We hear architects described as having built a building, as though they poured the concrete themselves. When work is excised like this, it is because it is devalued and considered to be low skilled. And the reasoning is circular: it is devalued because it is so easy to delete. This creates mistaken impressions of what work does in the world, and what it's like to do work. Work activities are far more interconnected and interdependent. Invisible and deleted work have to be recruited as ethical issues.

There is a history of feminist scholars who have tried to make non-existence visible, sometimes using the master's tools, to quote Audre Lorde,[13] for example, to understand western domestic work, and sometimes in broader ways. The troubled fate of a set of arguments that tried to stake a claim for the existence and importance of non-existent entities like unpaid work is instructive. It shows that arguments can be accepted and simultaneously ignored.

Making the domestic visible

The most invisible, the most hidden, the most often deleted work, is care work, especially that which happens in homes. Arguments for why domestic work matters were worked out in the 'domestic labour debates' held by Marxist and socialist feminists in the 1970s. These drew attention to how women's domestic work – whether paid or unpaid – contributed to capitalist systems by reproducing labour. Asserting the significance of gender inequality was an assertion of the limits of an overweening focus on class inequality. This discussion made visible the hidden work in the home, the work of housewives in cooking, cleaning and caring. 'Wages for housework' campaigns took the line that pay was a signal that work was valued. Even in the very idea of reproduction for paid work, 'economy first' positions are made: domestic work counts because it produces workers, not because of its contribution to love or comfort, or the transmission of culture. Capitalocentrism sees domestic activity through the lens of 'capitalist reproduction'.[14] From an 'economy first' point of view, households are subordinate to production. They are not amenable to the rationalisation in the manner of production lines, their messy intimacies are inefficient, and they do not directly produce stuff and so cannot produce value. But they re-make workers able to sell labour power. Back in 1984, Ray Pahl[15] said that the argument that domestic labour is work was won. But then, as now, the lesson hasn't been applied because of the complexity generated by thinking about 'work' in settings beyond paid employment. It ends up re-hidden.

A very brief history of global domestic service

Domestic service, that is, household work by non-family members, is another loose thread from the discussion of industrialisation in Chapter Two. Domestic service is a common occupation. It includes housework and care work and sometimes also includes agriculture and domestic production in some times and places. Studying it shows how (class) differences are made and maintained through who does the dirty work. As Jose Moya's[16] impressive survey of the global history of servants indicates, the quick assumptions engendered by the view from the Global North (that domestic service rises hand in hand with industrialisation and urbanisation, that it is feminised) is more complicated. For example, male domestic servants were preferred in Zimbabwe until the 1960s; the numbers and gender of servant workers is affected by local conditions (like being a frontier region, or there being a tourist economy). Feminisation is present, if not consistently, across time and place. Class differences are, as ever, intersectional with gender and race. For example, colonial British families employed Indian women as ayahs and wet nurses, and the memsahib was supposed to run her domestic set-up like a benevolent empress. But all kinds of 'colonial anxieties' run riot, in Indrani Sen's phrase:[17] who is judging whom, who is managing whom, what flows of feeling surround the care of children? The upshot of having women who did dirty work was that more privileged women – ornamental wives of bourgeois men – who did not engage in anything as sordid as scrubbing maintained social status. Where gender ideologies discourage women from engaging in public life, they also denigrate those who do paid work.

It can sometimes look like gender ideologies have magic powers. With fewer domestic servants and more domestic technologies in western homes by the 1950s, the housewife ideal seemed both ordinary and aspirational, women were invited to feel fulfilled by domestic work and celebrate being housewives. They got the dubious double bonus of being framed not as working but fulfilling natural urges by caring – morally valuable in the sense that it has to be done, but not valuable in the way that production is valuable. Not *economically* valuable, which in a capitalocentric world is the value that counts. The view from the west in the 20th century was that there was a shift from domestic service to care within families. That is one of those shorthand summaries that belies the complexity of interconnections of work. Domestic service persists globally, although its form varies. As I'll discuss in Chapter Six, live-in servants are still present. But more and more, domestic service is organised differently. Migrant entrepreneurs with small cleaning businesses provide domestic services; the presence or absence of welfare state provision affects how care is organised, and how it is recompensed, what technologies affect care provision. So, and obviously, how everyday life is lived is part and parcel of what care and service work is done.

Care as work

Domestic service and domestic labour refer to whether the work that happens in the home that maintains and repairs life is done by a paid outsider or an unpaid family member. (Other work based in the home will be discussed in Chapter Six.) Domestic work is not the same as, but overlaps with, care work. I move often between talking about domestic labour, domestic service, personal services and care. Each has different connotations, different assumptions about where work takes place and who does it. The terms are not synonyms at all, each laying stress on some different history and different feature of the work. How work is described and what it involves are both important to understanding what it is and what it does, and shifting between terms indicates the contingent and changeable ways that the work of maintaining life gets done, the institutions that might be involved, the practices and relations. Care work is especially interesting as it brings with it the connotations of care ethics discussed in Chapter One and so invites attention to questions of quality and feeling as well as organisation. If work is not collapsed into the specific category of paid, formal employment, then it gets all the more important to think about the modes of connection between and beyond work activities.[18] Once the lesson of not collapsing work into the specific category of paid, formal employment is learned, then new worlds, and new implications for ethics and politics, appear.

Extensive work, then, the work of life, involves looking after children, changing wound dressings and giving medicine, wiping down kitchen surfaces, picking up mess and organising schedules. Care work is often assumed to be low status and low skilled work, in part because of its naturalisation as women's work, but it is part of other kinds of work on bodies, such as that done by doctors. It is often intimate work, even when between strangers. It doesn't do to get all misty-eyed and soppy about care, as providing care does not mean being gentle or kind or careful. That the activity of working on someone or something to care for it, to maintain or repair it, can be done with or without affection, and carefully or carelessly, makes care a thick and complicated concept. The density of its reference points indicates some of the limits and problems that speaking simply of 'care work' or indeed 'care ethics' might have. Care might be a feature of doing work well expressed in the idea of doing something carefully, caring about another being. It can be a motivator for action, although 'motivator' somewhat reduces the complex ethical and emotional dynamics in doing care, as when feeling responsible means working carefully. It is worked out and negotiated.

As well as a way of thinking about working on and with human bodies, care also brings attention to the non-human, and hence to knots of both environment and technology. The care and repair of an environment in the face of far-reaching transformations of nature are certainly part of the agenda and scope of care – and this might be done carelessly, following assumptions that thinking humans apply environmental principles and act decisively on a passive nature, or carefully, following what Maria Puig de la Bellacasa[19] describes as a kind of 'decentred obligation' to accept the transformative effects (for good and for bad) of ordinary and everyday practices.

What concepts for understanding work might have been developed if domestic service was taken as the exemplary form of labour in the 19th century, rather than factory work? And what would happen if care work, not industrial production, was the start of understanding work? Certainly, questions of power, control and class would have a more intimate nuance to them, and that might mean isolation at work meant more than class-based collectivities. The comparatively small scale of service is important: small numbers of servants, perhaps only one, employed at each home/workplace. Status hierarchies within and between households affect what domestic service is like; mechanisms of control and punishment are personalised and emotional. This points to a politics of work that attends to personhood as well as position in relation to the means of production.

Making care and service visible is a political act, recognising that being hidden in private and intimate spaces affects the ethical and political issues for those involved. Putting care at the heart makes some kinds of reasoning impossible. Because care labour is not always wage labour, concepts that rely on seeing ownership, extraction of value and power as the only source of inequalities need some significant refining. Capitalocentric reasoning would say that all these activities are merely ways in which labour forces are reproduced, except that how care and service happens has sensory, aesthetic, ethical and emotional resonances that won't slip down the 'it's all economy' funnel. Care brings different, multiple kinds of relations into view. Sometimes it is organised through a wage relationship, at other times through family ties. Different dynamics of power and exploitation are involved. As care/work means giving attention to others (human and non-human), it invites thinking about responsiveness to other beings, and so it gives rise to an ethics and politics of work which need not be limited to thinking about the body of the worker. It's impossible to think about care without seeing humans as connected, with each other and with other beings.

Technologies of care

The persistent presence of domestic labour, domestic service work and care work is a counterpoint to celebrations of the glorious fourth industrial revolution, when AI will take over work. That's not to say that care exists on a separate track from stories about technology (as in, for example, caring robots), or about environment (pollution creates a greater need for care), but only to point out that constant presence problematises linear projections of constant progress. Housework gets a bit easier when people are more insulated from nature through (now mundane) technologies and infrastructures, whether through access to easy light and heat, or to having water come to them instead of them having to go and get it. Laundry was the first chore American women would try to get rid of if they had the money.[20] Hand laundry is hard work: all that boiling, scrubbing, rinsing and wringing. They sent it to washerwomen, and then used commercial laundries and mechanical aids. Commercial laundries were important in the development of washing machine technology, but when washing machines started to be mass produced/mass consumed, then laundry returned to the home. It does look like less effort is needed when machines substitute for human labour: washing machines are easier than scrubbing with river water. There is, however, often a 'more work for mother' effect, to quote the title of Ruth Schwartz Cowan's book,[21] as standards of cleanliness change. Further, arguments about simple technological substitution erase the effort that is still needed. There is work at the point of use – being responsible, operating the machine and doing all the other tasks that the machine doesn't do, managing other people's work and not getting irritated by having responsibility. There is also work to bring the technology to the home – to design, build, sell and transport the goods with which the 'end user' has such an easy time. Bringing care to mind when thinking about technologies makes for a more complicated reading of technology, because it knots together feeling and the action that makes the world. It makes me think about whether the design of technologies captures orientations to care (does the doctor look at the patient or at the screen?), and about how repair and maintenance happen.

Commodification, care and service

In getting this far in the argument, I have had to talk about gender. 'Gendering the analysis' means taking seriously the work that happens in domestic settings, including care for family members, which is more likely to be done by women even in countries with gender equality.[22] It also means thinking about women's and men's paid and unpaid work of all kinds, the jobs they do and how they do them. And when analysis is gendered it should also be racialised and ethnicised, in order to recognise how gender, class and race intersect with migration status, age and childcare responsibilities, sexual and gender identities to affect people's experience of the world. Doing this makes it easier to avoid essentialising the ideas that women always do care work, that women should do care work, or that all women are the same, wherever. To my mind this is an important way of showing that inequalities of work are not only explainable through the lens of social class. An example: hotel workers in the Global North are often recent migrants. In London hotels, workers are of many different nationalities. Managers often used the gender of the worker to decide on where to place them (women as cleaners, men as kitchen porters), and also made assumptions about the 'natural advantages' of some nationalities over others. Cultural stereotyping and racism were reinforced when managers used their own assumptions about customers' preferences to justify segregation.[23]

Domestic spaces provided the start of my argument in this chapter, but the kinds of life-sustaining care activities that happen there transcend domestic spaces. They can be called care, but they are often also personal service work. At the start of the chapter, I talked about how concepts create exclusions. In this section, the overlap and distinctions between 'care' and 'service' matter. Fast food and dental hygiene are more than frivolous status signals in a consumer society, more than mundane forms of consumption that reproduce the worker and get them back to their workstation. They are also kinds of care work, and indicate how service work is oriented to maintaining bodies. The recently emerging web platforms that match workers to service consumers – taxi services, help with small tasks, food delivery, among others – have often been discussed through the lens of technology, especially that these platform technologies radically change the way we work. I think that something else is going on, and that exploring the overlaps between care and service are the way to see it.

Three features of how ordinary self-care relies on service work interest me in particular. The first is that people eat. No prizes for stating the obvious, I know, but stay with me. Cooking at home from scratch, part of bourgeois morality for Global North middle classes, relies on an assemblage of skill, technology, consumption and time. It requires a kitchen with a gas or electricity supply. In Taiwan, people eat out a lot.[24] Which came first: the small kitchen or the reluctance to boil an egg? It's normal to eat dinner out in Taiwan, where working hours are long and there are large numbers of small traders selling cheap, hot food. The work of living, the work that makes worlds, is variable. The second is that in the face of work intensification, or indeed other changes to paid work, the form of service/care changes. Perhaps it is more extensive than it was, as some who talk about the new gig economy imply. The third is how state provision of care and services affect what people pay for and what they get others to do for free. I'll think about these latter two in detail now; the first will be discussed in Chapter Six.

Gig work is old work

When people talk about 'the gig economy', they are usually referring to two ways of organising work. One, crowdwork (organisations use online platforms to source people willing to do specific tasks, with Amazon's Mechanical Turk being the most well-known platform). Two, and closer to the theme of this chapter, 'work on-demand via apps', where consumers wanting help with everyday tasks are put in touch with workers.[25] The gig economy now is connected to the prevalence of service and care work of different kinds, and of the appearance and disappearance of markets affecting how everyday life is lived. Service platforms used by gig-consumers are a public version of long-private care work. Gig work apps often provide domestic services such as food provisioning, transport, DIY help and other personal services. Put like that, the technological present and future is hooked into the knot of care, and into how and when care/services are made into commodities.

In all the talk of the 'game changer' that is the 'platform society' it is easy to stop noticing those kinds of work that exceed or are not captured and subsumed by digital technologies. The other danger is to overstate the newness of the phenomenon. Informal work is globally and historically the most common form of work (Chapter Six will take this discussion forward). Full employment is neither a historical nor a geographical norm; it's an exception.[26] It was part of an approximately 30-year period of comparative consensus and agreement between workers (represented by unions), states and corporations in the 1950s to the 1970s in west Europe, closely associated with the post-war settlement. It's connected to the cultural idea of a breadwinner wage (alongside unequal pay and prohibitions on married women having paid jobs), which encourages the idea that men's work (often in industrial production) counts most. The paid work that women do gets downgraded; it becomes work for 'pin money' or work that women don't deserve to have. It is constituted by associations between women, home, care and feeling. Now, this well-protected status group who reaped all kinds of benefits is no longer so well protected. Work for the former labour aristocracy is now much more similar to the globally common phenomena of extensive insecurity at work.

If you slice the historical cake differently, the current moment of an emerging gig economy stops seeming like an aberration from this norm of full employment for male breadwinners. The gig economy has its historical echoes in men showing up to dockyards at the start of the day hoping to get picked, in women getting jobs and 'proving' their citizenship during wars but then being sacked when soldiers return looking for work, and in the category of 'office temp' recruited through an agency. The racialised and gendered reserve army of labour may now be whiter and more male and more educated than it has been. Gig work, in relation to the unpredictability of working hours and working time, and therefore of pay, is so ordinary that it is surprising that it ever seems new and shocking.

It's easy to think that technology drives the change to the gig economy, and certainly there wouldn't be a gig economy without the platforms. But that kind of reasoning doesn't go very far in making sense of service apps. The decades of softening up, so that the norm of full employment is remoulded into normalised flexibility, contributes to both a shift in likely demand for gig work services as long and unpredictable working hours take their toll. And the apps would only work if there was a workforce to provide them, that is to say, in the absence of less precarious work. In this sense, technology is assembled through and with social and economic realities, and the flexibility of work and consumption that are the essence of the gig economy are part of a long historical process. I think that historical process can best be understood by thinking about gig work in relation to the gendering and racialisation of care/service work. Slow-cooked casualisation, a 'crisis in care', the end of breadwinner/homemaker models are the context for gig apps as much as the software-bros who design the apps, or the venture capitalists who concoct the market. Substituting service provided by maid, mother or wife, gig apps cook and deliver food, arrange for a cleaner to come around, and give lifts into work. The working conditions of gig workers now are poor because the work they do – gendered and racialised care work and service work – has long been devalued, deleted and made invisible.

Private worlds and public spheres

Private worlds are entwined with public worlds. I used the example of markets that provide consumer services in the previous section. In this section, the way that nation-states affect how care is done is the theme – different kinds of care offered through different modes in different times and places. Care is often part of public policy, most obviously through healthcare and associated services. Often economic reasoning is used to legitimate these kinds of policies, as when state spending on health is justified because a healthy workforce contributes to economic growth. The same song sheet has the lyrics for justifying immigration solely of skilled care workers able to address the care deficit for an ageing population. It's an instance of the resurgent power of historical inequalities between majority and minority worlds. This economy-first reasoning spreads far and wide. Might it be possible to speak differently and turn up the volume on other kinds of justifications, for example, to shout loudly about making a liveable and rich life?

Some years ago, I was part of a project that argued for 'a new sociology of work', one that would recognise the interconnections of different kinds of work, including paid and unpaid work.[27] Since then, I've thought more about how framing the question affects the answer, and I've learned since then that our arguments didn't go far enough. I want to undelete, and question, our western-centric assumptions. Rebecca Taylor, one of my co-authors, now says how the categories of paid and unpaid, formal and informal that were important to us then are more fragmented now. Care services can be a hybrid of voluntary work, unpaid work, state provision and family and community support. In the case of formally provided services, new public management (NPM), outsourcing and subcontracting have changed how work is organised and its modes of interconnection. People working in one building, apparently for the same organisation, have different employers, different conditions of work. People doing nominally the same job, even, are paid differently and treated differently in New York parks.[28] Volunteers are more important (and more privileged in every way) than all the other groups, but especially those doing unfree work.

The greater fragmentation of state service provision has happened in places where technocratic common sense is that outsourcing public services to private companies is best. The UK is a leader in this. Indeed, the NPM movement encourage non-profit organisations to become more business-like, importing private sector norms and financial procedures into welfare services; charities have the accoutrements, including financial portfolios and brand positions, of private sector organisations. Of the many effects this has, I'll mention three in particular. First, the way some governments walk away from provision of services and leave them to markets (always differently, in different places). For example, private sector provision of government services (for example, in response to disasters such as hurricane Katrina in the US in 2005) creates markets for humanitarian relief. It reconfigures those affected by disaster as deserving of help when they act in entrepreneurial ways, and don't seem to be desperate enough for handouts. This is crony capitalism, making money from welfare states on the back of contracts that incentivise the private corporation to take a long time to avoid handing out much money to those in need.[29]

Second, it denies or makes difficult the idea that those who work in health and care may do so because they are committed to care. Such workers may well be suspicious of management philosophies that encourage technological solutions or entrepreneurialism, and they may struggle to do good work under conditions where profit-making companies want to cut corners so as to cut costs. Labour costs are prime targets for cost reduction. Outsourcing care services is a deliberate strategy to invisibilise work, and to make working conditions and the quality of the care work done no longer anyone's responsibility.

Third, and least well recognised, is that changing how public services are provided changes both the service and the capacity of the state to engage effectively (and on an equal footing) with the private actors. In a study of UK local government, initial cost savings and gains in flexibility in one such study, which were referred to as 'trimming the fat' of work practices dominated by entrenched labour interests,[30] were not sustained;

comparing and verifying competitor bids was long and expensive. Note here how fear of organised labour explicitly motivates the reorganisation. Outsourcing state provision meant a loss of expertise within the civil service.[31] The regular turnover of contract management staff, for example, left knowledge gaps in the civil service that private sector companies could exploit by 'training' up the new civil service staff in modes of thought favourable to the private company. So, outsourcing has an effect on the organisation of the work of governance, as well as (even because of) on the workers whose contracts are moved.

Why hidden work matters

Care foregrounds connection, trust, relationships and mutual dependence, as well as tension and worry. It makes me think that the ethics and politics of work can't just be a question of the ethical treatment of workers, but of the ethics of what work does, and how it is done. How does care happen? I don't discuss care in order to replace other kinds of ethical concerns, but as a way to think about what parts of work are hidden and deleted, that is, to think about the ethics and politics of work in relation to Fassin's 'worthless rock' of doing work (see Chapter One). Care is contested and contradictory and that is why it is an interesting concept to think with in relation to the struggle to find ways of thinking about the ethics and politics of work. How work gets done is the subject of the next chapter.

Assuming that paid work is the work that counts hides many other kinds of work. Assuming that factory work is the norm makes a claim that this work, and these workers, matter more. Both assumptions hide and delete other work, especially care work. Making this more visible generates new ideas for what counts for the ethics and politics of work – care, relationality and a clearer sense of how work makes the world. Starting to notice invisible work gives rise to an ethics of recognition. The misrecognition of wage labour means that it is not properly valued; the misrecognition of other work means that it doesn't even get called work.

The cultural presence of the ideal of paid work (consider, for example, paid work as the route out of poverty, paid work as the route out of gendered familial oppressions, paid work as the route out of stigmatisation as a scrounger) might make it seem like the thing that matters then is to study paid work. In my mind, it creates more demand for insights into how other kinds of work are organised: the work that is interwoven with paid employment. Policies that affect work are part of this story, such as when welfare that is tied to doing paid work (as in Germany's 'one-euro job' scheme) or when young workers migrate to cities for factory work in China so that rural villages are hollowed out. Who cares, and how they care, has then to be worked out. I suggest that the economic policies directed at labour markets, corporations and welfare are tied to intimate politics, including the politics of inequalities in homes and communities. Work has never been reducible to paid, public work.

FOUR

How does a body work?

Introduction

The road outside my house acquired some new potholes last
winter. If your job is to repair potholes, then your ability to
do that is a composition of the skills you have, the materials at
play, the weather and road use, the underlying soil structure,
how pothole repair is (or is not) funded, the effectiveness of
the private contractor or local government repair team that
employ you. Many factors affect how long that repair will last.
In this chapter, I think about what work does in the world.
I will argue that we understand work better when we think
about encounters with machines, with non-human others (soil,
animals, weather) as well as with human others (colleagues,
managers and customers) and with institutions. This greater
insight comes from paying attention to the mundane and
ordinary practices of bodies doing work in order to see how
the world is shaped by work. From that, it is possible to ask
questions about the normative implications of how work is
done. That is because we bring into view the way ethics and
politics are lived and felt in bodies, in the body of the worker
and in how work changes the world. I try to avoid the omissions
engendered by ethical theorising that takes the human out of
the world. I think with and against ideas of dignity. Dignity at
work places an apparently universal human figure at the front
and centre of its reasoning. Rethinking dignity with a more
rounded account of the assemblage of work makes for a more
sensitive account of what bodies do when they work.

I do this by extending the idea of invisible and hidden work through a focus on materiality. That is, to thinking about how matter – objects and things, human and non-human – shapes and is shaped by social and cultural encounters. I will look at taken-for-granted infrastructures and technologies that provide the conditions for work, but which often seem invisible when trying to understand work. New technologies get introduced in order to forget a problem, so it can stop being a problem. But these technologies create problems. This discussion is an essential part of my argument about the importance of technology, environment and work. I also look at the matter and mattering of human bodies as they do work, discussing skill, craft and emotion in work to consider: what does a body do when it works? What does it use and what does it shape?

Dignity

Dignity is a charismatic ethical concept that invites thinking about how human bodies are controlled and constrained but also enabled in work. Dignity is a marker of a shared humanity in much western political philosophy, including that which informs human rights discourses. Human dignity is only possible when humans have freedom and autonomy, and that implies also that they have equality, and respect and esteem from others. Dignity is based on a dualism between human and non-human, where the human is defined through his ability to act freely and be rational. These are the grounds on which he deserves human dignity. I say 'his' quite deliberately, because in some practices, it's not always clear that women always have an equal right to this human dignity. Autonomy, specifically the autonomy to make choices, is the honoured entry in that list of abstract concepts that make up dignity. Autonomy relies on human specialness because of this same ability to reason freely, as an individual. Co-dependencies and feelings don't matter that much: the lessons of care ethics have not been learned. Dignity-as-autonomy deletes the relations and interconnections between work and life and so it gets easy to claim that actions that sit within the web of everyday interdependencies are actually autonomous. There's one exception: the dignity concept takes

70

very seriously the hierarchical relationship between managerial control and would-be autonomous worker. Management hierarchies are a threat to dignity.

Dignity and work

The idea of dignity brings with it some contradictions, including between the laudable normative intention of promoting human dignity through support for justice and rights, with the uncertain social (in)dignities of those groups of people who are not granted dignity. This contradiction is especially complicated in paid work, because as soon as someone is contracted to work for another, they give up some autonomy. They are managed; they are constrained to spend a certain amount of time in doing set tasks. In this sense, dignity is impossible because there is no autonomy. This position reflects arguments discussed in Chapter Two that consider industrial work as degrading and unpleasant and offering only the pleasure of resisting control. And yet work is not only an assault on dignity; it is a potentially resource for dignity. This idea is often expressed as 'meaningful work' of the kind that offers intrinsic rewards, and also relates to how work and life are balanced so that life *outside* work is meaningful (for example, that provides enough money and leaves enough time and energy for a fulfilling leisure or family life).

Sharon Bolton[1] distinguishes between dignity in work and dignity at work. The former refers to autonomy and esteem and to doing work that is interesting and meaningful. The latter refers to how a worker is treated, and includes respect and equality in how employment is organised. Employment conditions (including pay and other kinds of reward), security, precariousness and desirable flexibility, hours of work, training, voice, representation and participation, health and safety, accidents, stress and burnout, risks including job loss are part of this second element, and will be discussed in Chapter Five. I'll focus more in this chapter on dignity in work, that is, on what the work itself demands of the worker. Some of these elements of dignity are inherent to how work is organised. For example, it's hard to work well in a badly organised workplace. Other elements of dignity can be earned, for example, when work is meaningful work.

Randy Hodson,[2] who followed a quite unusual methodology of studying the texts produced by social scientists (here, ethnographers of [factory] work), argues that there are four 'faces' to dignity. These are: first, mismanagement and abuse, where work is poorly organised in ways that make it hard to do a good job, and managers are controlling or aggressive; second, overwork, which can result from the pace of work being too fast, the quantity of work excessive and/or the hours of work too long to enable the worker to live well; third, limits to autonomy, as when non-experts intervene in the work of experts (hospital managers changing how clinical staff operate, or new software systems extract different kinds of work); and fourth, contradictory attempts to involve employees in decision-making, which includes contemporary managerial practices such as performance management to bring workers into line with corporate culture. Employee involvement is not inherently problematic; it can contribute to dignity if workers' views and ideas are heard. The problem comes when it makes workers responsible for situations which they cannot reasonably help. An example is the fake autonomy on offer in some British banks. Employees are told that they are empowered, but only insofar as they are made responsible for conforming to set standards and hierarchies.[3]

The ideas about dignity focus on the lifeworld of the worker, but not about what work does in the world. David Hesmondhalgh and Sarah Baker[4] have pointed out that creative workers' commitment to what they do or to what they make is a dimension of good work. I think this is key to an expanded ethics and politics of work, developing the ideas around Question 3, what work does in the world. That's not to say that workers always have choices (as the autonomous, dignified worker would do) to do something good, but that there is productive potential in imagining work as having effects in the world and thinking about what those effects should be.

What's wrong with dignity?

In Chapter One I talked about how principles of justice for all humans is something of an illusion, and unfree labour (see

Chapter Two) made this all the more real. The similarity of dignity to the conquering, apparently universal, ethical concept of justice gives reasons to quibble with 'dignity'. When First Nations peoples are not accorded the same human rights and hence dignity as settler people in legal statutes; when brand directors and consumers know that the clothes they buy were made by workers locked into factories without safe fire exits; when care work is deemed easy, or natural for women and so made invisible, then some humans are excluded from the category 'universal human' and effectively denied rights and dignity. Dignity and justice are unevenly applied in the world. They claim to be universal, but they are specific and exclude as they include. The risk is that western white male experiences are privileged by the assumption that they are the archetype of a universal human.

One of the problems with creating frameworks such as 'dignity in and at work' is that it contains contradictions. Where routine work is secure but tedious, or creative work provides autonomy but is precarious, then what constitutes 'dignity' is not obvious.[5] By operating with a universal human, dignity at work leaves implicit (at best) recognition of the effect of social inequalities of gender, race and class on work. Further, the relationship between work and other elements of life is not well considered by researchers thinking with dignity – neither (paid) work–life balance, nor career progression are encapsulated. For example, tightly controlled (undignified) factory work has an important and perhaps positive effect on the life of the worker – women get freedom and autonomy outside work, if not within work.[6]

On the one hand, dignity ideas make it possible to recognise how new technology affects dignity in and at work – as when call centre technology speeds up work by sending a new call to a worker as soon as they've hung up on the last one, and when it monitors and assesses performance on the basis of calculations of break times, speed of the call and so on. On the other hand, I am not sure that this goes far enough in thinking about the interdependences of human and non-human entities. Being mostly concerned with how humans treat other humans – how managers treat workers, for example

– technology and other non-human entities become a proxy through which management power can be understood. The ghostly processes through which work comes to be designed and organised, assumptions about the production of value that affect how managers understand work and manage employees, the issue of what counts as expertise in different settings and what that does, and the tools and techniques of management and corporate cultures all make me think about quite a lot of other questions that need to be asked in order to understand dignity in work. What are the infrastructures on which this work relies? What kinds of space is work done in, and how is it affected by nature and environment? Without these questions, 'dignity' is an intense abstraction and we cannot really understand how dignity is ever achieved or not achieved. So much is missing, so much has been deleted.

So for as long as dignity is taken as an intuitive and broad universal idea, yet another concept that it's hard to be against, and when the shared dignity of humans is the foundation for an ethics of the human, then it seems powerful. The dignity of individuals becomes a political question as it opens up questions about the nature of justice, democracy and equality. The attraction of dignity at work for me is how it invites interest in the messy details of how work is done. But as I read the dignity research, I find that it summons ghosts. It takes so much for granted, that dignity is clear enough to make sense, that dignity rests on the direct actions of humans, and that the invisible, hidden or deleted work discussed in Chapter Three on which visible work depends doesn't matter so much. What new thinking is needed to expand those ideas?

Assembling infrastructures, organisations and bodies

The idea of the assemblage invites better thinking about dignity and work by extending the question of the ethics of what bodies do, from the concerns about human exceptionalism, so present in the idea of dignity, to the more general concern of how interconnections between forms of work make the world. Assemblages of different kinds of entities – objects, beings and words, for example – come together to make some actions possible. Assemblage thinking can give a more comprehensive insight into desirable dignity when it invites 'nature' in to the conversation. That helps to overcome the separation (dualism) between human and non–human. Assemblage challenges the assumptions of Enlightenment philosophy that nature is passive and inert in the face of active human culture. That challenge restarts a conversation about work, and about how bodies do work. Take that most banal of conversation topics, the weather. It seems too ordinary to bother with, just a background grumble to everyday life. But weather is part of work. It is there when it's too hot to concentrate, or too cold to grip a tool properly; it is there when a drought makes getting water harder; it is there in seasonal work when crops ripen or when snowy roads need clearing. It changes as climates change. Other natural entities and beings are also assembled through work. Pest control sprayers are active against insurgent insects threatening crops; engineers and builders look at soil and bedrock when setting building foundations.

When economic activity can only see nature as a resource for human use, it makes it seem controllable, extractable at will. That way of thinking ignores the unpredictability of natural beings and forces. Solutionism also provides an incentive to delete or deny nature. For example, solar panels, which are a 'solution' to the crisis in energy generation, need photovoltaic cells made of minerals that are extracted from processed metal ores. The damage to extraction and processing workers and the environments in which they work has to be denied in order for solar panels to retain their place as a solution. I'll talk more about the contradictions of extraction work and environment in Chapter Eight.

Doing work relies on infrastructures that are so taken for granted that they end up seeming to be invisible. Assemblage thinking brings these out into the open, and that, in turn, draws attention to an important way that work makes the world. Infrastructures, including water and electricity, roads and railways, sewers and mobile phone networks, 'reside in a naturalised background, as ordinary and unremarkable to us as trees, daylight, and dirt'.[7] All these infrastructures, whether relating to control of the natural world or to everyday provisioning, rely on organised work, and make other work possible. They channel and constrain forces. This creates engagements, relationships, effects and feelings.

It is not magic dust that keeps infrastructures going; it is work that creates, maintains and repairs infrastructures. This work is affected by what's normal in different places, by who owns and is responsible for the infrastructure (the state or a private company), and what work it takes for people to make use of the infrastructure. The form that infrastructure takes affects how other work is done. It affects other paid work, and it affects domestic work. Infrastructure may be taken for granted, but it is fully a part of everyday social life. Abdou Maliq Simone describes this nicely: 'People work on things to work on each other, as these things work on them.'[8]

Noticing infrastructure is a way to see how life is made, to see what other work depends on, and to understand the interconnections of different kinds of work. There are techniques that make it possible to undo the deletion of infrastructure work. One is to look at what happens when infrastructures break down as then they become not just noticeable but also overwhelmingly important. Breakdowns require repair, and that demands work and causes disruptions. Seeing roadworks on my commute to work, or trying to work out the changes to train times caused by engineering works, is a reminder, though, that disruptions to infrastructure are often not aberrations, but (annoyingly) ordinary. Another technique is to look at what outsiders think and notice. The social power of infrastructures is on display when an outsider takes a while to work out how things are done. This is the kind of learning that people do visiting a new city, or when new in a job. It takes know-how, as well as formal training. It takes tacit knowledge. These techniques are examples of a method of 'infrastructural inversion' advocated by Bowker and Star. Infrastructural inversion is 'a struggle against the tendency of infrastructure to disappear (except when breaking down). It means learning to look closely at technologies and arrangements that, by design and by habit, tend to fade into the woodwork'.[9] The effect is to acknowledge work, not merely as the production of consumer goods, or the care of human bodies, but as activities on which other work and other life depends. Infrastructural inversion reveals normally invisible threads and connections, and although these may become quickly ordinary, mundane and start to hide themselves in among the day-to-day tensions and challenges of work, they nonetheless can be brought back to mind by thinking what this work, task, role, activity relies on that can't be seen right now. For example, infrastructures to categorise and arrange information are designed and managed; they are not accidental. This is work done by IT workers that sets boundaries on knowledge.

It may seem a long way from the ideas of human dignity that started this chapter, but the capacious understanding of the materials that make life possible, that are worked on and that make other work possible, that affect others' capacity to work, is an undercurrent to thinking about the ethics of work. That people work with tools and technologies that are part of infrastructures is part of an important story about the *materiality* of work environments and the materiality of human bodies doing work.

Being interested in photocopiers

One of my favourite studies that explores how work gets done is Julian Orr's *Talking about machines.*[10] This study makes it so clear how work relies on work, and shows the contingency and fuzziness of work. Ordinary and old-fashioned technologies like photocopiers still matter despite the promise of paperless offices and cloud computing. They are produced via the kinds of global branding and supply chain processes talked about in Chapter Two, and used in offices to make other work activities possible. So the repair work to fix them matters to whatever work is done in the organisation that rents that machine. Orr trailed round with people (mostly men) employed by the photocopier manufacturer to mend photocopiers in other organisations, and heard the stories they told about fixing machines. Photocopiers are part of the ordinary machinery of office life, and they have a tendency to break down. Even 'standardised' machines are not entirely standard. Orr found that mending them demanded that the repairers improvise with possible solutions. They had to be skilled in reading the machines, working on them, hearing what other people said about them, and talking about them. The technicians worked with customers and machines, and also drew on each other's knowledge and understandings (of specific machines, of typical problems and possible solutions). The problems require slow diagnosis and experimentation to find solutions.

Like many other kinds of work, mending machines is contingent and skilled. It relies on an embodied encounter with the machine being repaired, as well as with clients, colleagues, managers, guidance literature and even the city traffic that the engineers negotiate when moving between call-outs; it is the basis on which other work is possible. A department without a photocopier can't operate its standard routines. This points to the power of ordinary technologies in routine working lives. This tells me that the boundaries between kinds of work are fuzzy, and that material technologies, working or breaking down, condition how work is done.

Technology design

One of the implications of the 'work is production' research strand discussed in Chapter Two, related as it is to an understanding of work that separates mental and manual labour, is that it imagines the central tension in work to be that of control and management. All of the features of Hodson's ideas about dignity (mismanagement and abuse; overwork; limits to autonomy through job design and employee involvement) are questions of management and control. In this way of thinking, the design of work technologies and tools has a single and simple rationale: make production efficient and hence profitable, often by reducing workers' capacities to decide for themselves how to do something. This is the principle of deskilling that Braverman talked about. Technorationalisation is assumed to be right in line with profit maximisation. Technologies, therefore, are embedded with invisible controls intended to control labour, considered to be a homogenous mass, not a group of thinking, able individuals. Production lines and automatic call routing in call centres are examples of work tools which are designed to inhibit workers' autonomous actions.

When faceless and unspecified 'managers' are assumed to be able to roll out new technologies and control their implementation with the aim of deskilling work, and where response *on the ground* is read only in terms of resistance to undifferentiated power, then the impact on work of new technology is only partly understood. Technologies seem to be unveiled as natural, inevitable and fixed. In my view, talk about technology has a performative effect similar to the kind of effect that talk about 'The Economy' has (as discussed in Chapter One). It seems real, external and powerful, running according to its own agenda harnessable only by management as a tool for power and control. I think it is contingent, immanent and unpredictable, and that thinking differently about it reveals new ways of considering dignity, and new ways of thinking about the ethics of work. The purchase of new software, say, reshapes a firm when workers have to negotiate their way around the changes which the software brings. Such negotiations carry with them both questions about technologies and infrastructures, and the assumption, for right or wrong, that technologies and infrastructures can solve a problem.

Key to this alternative way of thinking about technology is understanding the work that goes into the design of technologies and devices. Even a tool designed for a specific work activity brings with it more than just the solution to an articulated problem. Tools contain cultural assumptions (for example, about how things are always done or about what can be done); they have histories and type-forms. They have unintended effects – perhaps they break down in unanticipated ways; perhaps they don't work in intended ways. In the case of the failed automated car production line at Tesla, they do not create promised efficiencies because machines are less flexible than the human bodies which they replaced.[11] If technology design is understood through a specific lens (of deskilling, of efficiency), these other features get deleted. Thinking with Susan Leigh Star's ideas about deleted labour (from Chapter Three) and infrastructural inversion, a different angle emerges. Design reflects the way that knowledge (for example, of how to do a task) is distributed. Knowledge gets captured into technologies, and gets codified and solidified through design. That sets constraints on what can be done and how it can be done: design expertise is assembled into the technology, and that then assembles some activities as possible and others as not. What gets included? What gets ignored? Design work is world building. The design and development of an app for taxi services draws on cultural assumptions that flexible work is acceptable and creates new practices for workers and consumers. In Chapter Seven, I'll take this discussion further to see some more limits to the apparently undeniable promise that useful technologies can translate nuanced and contingent work processes into technorational systems. For now, I will say that machines and technologies designed to substitute work do not straightforwardly capture the hidden work contained in the tacit knowledge of workers, despite the assumptions commonly made about technology's reach. This kind of assembling of expertise lies behind apparently fixed and clear structures. To put it another way, work mediates economic change and organisational change. Organisations are made through their activities.

Bodies that work

Both managerial control and the material and technical arrangement of work constrain the autonomy of workers to think and act. Understanding both matters to understanding dignity, but is not all that counts. That work is embodied is one of those observations that seems too banal to even say. Of course, doing work needs/relies on a body. Sometimes, though, it's useful to say what's obvious, and examine the features of the obvious that are taken for granted. What do human bodies do when they work, and how does that shape issues of autonomy and dignity?

In other writing[12] I have considered embodied labour as an incorporation of other people, material environments, tools and technologies in order to make sense of the effort of doing work. Tim Ingold's[13] understanding of skilled practice as making interventions in among the flows of other entities in the world makes good sense to me. Working with other entities – human and non-human – involves committing to judgement and discrimination as to how to do something. Doing work is thereby an embodied process where material bodies, tools and techniques are entwined. Thinking about embodied labour draws attention to anticipation, understanding and awareness of self and others. It indicates the importance of sensory, aesthetic and emotional entanglements to how work is done, and I think that these entanglements are important to thinking about dignity, and to thinking about the three ethical questions that matter to my understanding of what's wrong with work.

Craft work

Recent revivals in thinking about craft as somehow a more authentic way to work than doing office work or factory work are nostalgic, and pretty narrow in how they think about work.[14] They tend not to think much about care and body work. I am not a fan of this nostalgic vision of craft work as good work, but I do think that craft is an interesting topic for how it shows that work is contingent. When someone learns a job, that learning changes them. Bodies are changed through practice; some muscles get strengthened, some abilities get honed. Newbies and amateurs don't have the same body that the capable worker has. Soldiers have to relearn how to breathe.[15] This is not 'autonomy', that central feature of dignity. It is competency: a body trained and harnessed to operate in a particular way. When Dawn Lyon and Les Back[16] describe how fishmongers learn how to weigh by eye and assess quality by feel, in order to work quickly, they describe this kind of bodily transformation; it is also what Berner[17] is talking about when he describes the work of tender manipulation which it takes to get and keep a machine going. Bodies are unpredictable, though, and highly skilled is not always highly competent – imagine a tired surgeon or a nervous space scientist. Having a delicate touch can't be taken for granted.

Embodied capabilities are also codified, transmitted and translated in many ways. Explaining a patient's illness to them is not the same as performing surgery on the patient, nor the same as negotiating with other healthcare workers over treatment, nor with writing up a treatment protocol that other medical staff might use. It's not the same as talking to a trainee surgeon, who learns by having actions described to them and then trying them out. Many kinds of lower status work rely on dexterity and concentration, on working bodies that have honed skills over time. Despite the lists which policy-makers write of the skills which are needed to make a workforce 'competitive in a global economy', skills are rarely finite, definable and graspable bundles. They are more specific, more contingent, more related to events and situations. They are woven together. Technical and social skills are needed to be a hairdresser; different technical and different social skills are needed to be a soldier, fishmonger or factory worker. The misrecognition of skills, their naturalisation – as in the cliché of the 'nimble-fingered' and mild-mannered female Malaysian factory worker,[18] contributes to the economic and social devaluation of some kinds of work. Skill and craft capabilities and judgements are assembled in organisations, in times and places. For example, when international agencies such as the IMF and World Bank set conditions for their intervention that national economies have to be 'opened up', local experts get retrained in order to work differently. But such translation practices are not straightforward.

Recognising skill and craft, and the challenge of learning how to work, contributes to rethinking the ethics of work. It draws attention to the experience of doing work, including to feeling the pains of repetitive activity, and it makes the contingency of work situations – where, for example, the objects that workers encounter (humans, non-humans) respond in unpredictable/ different ways, where training, tacit knowledge and the expectations of others affect how the work gets done – much clearer. Encounters with other humans are a really important part of this.

Encountering other people

'Body work' that involves touching other people's bodies[19] risks far deeper assaults on dignity, because of the many forms of status inequality that are involved, as hinted at in Chapter Three's discussion of how care is gendered and racialised. In factories, bodies suffer pains from working on the line, and from being controlled by manager and machine, but these are not the same pains that come from body work. Care workers, masseurs, hairdressers, all kinds of personal service providers, as well as the full array of medical workers, have intimate encounters with strangers. They develop ways of doing this, often drawing on professional norms that are supposed to 'maintain the dignity' of all parties. That's not so straightforward. Body work is always a response to the specifics of the person being worked on. This work is, like mending photocopiers, contingent on the problem in front of them. Second, the idea of dignity is based on the independence and autonomy of the human, and that forgets or ignores the relationality between people which is at the very heart of the work. Encountering another's body changes the boundaries of the human. More obviously than work with machines, body work and personal service work involves and evokes feeling, and the control and management of feeling. Comparable contingencies are present in other kinds of service work too.

My way of thinking about doing work stresses the contingent, unpredictable and singular, and this points to the difficulty of finding simple solutions to what's wrong with work. The involvement of clients and customers in work is a gigantic source of that contingency. As William F. Whyte said 70 years ago, 'When workers and customers meet ... that relationship adds a new dimension to the pattern of human relations in industry.'[20] That is an insight that keeps on giving. Emotional labour is the concept that really makes sense of encountering customers. It originated in Arlie Hochschild's research into flight attendants and debt collectors,[21] and refers to the way in which workers are expected to manage their own emotions in order to create feelings in customers. To do this, they might engage in shallow acting – smiling without meaning it – or deep acting, *really* feeling like they want to help. This kind of emotional performance alienates workers from their own feelings. It is extracted by managerial control, and by customers. It is gendered and racialised because of cultural expectations about natural ways to behave. A worker's sense of themselves and ability to look, feel and act is central to them getting and keeping work, and to producing other people's leisure and consumer lives.

Emotional labour has been used to think about service work, creative work and professional work, where interaction between a worker and a customer, client, or patient is central. Working with unpredictable others, where training, craft skills, technical systems and discourses create and reinforce social hierarchies – the means through which the customer is made to be always right. The waiter expected to have an outgoing personality, the call centre operative expected to take racist insults, the freelance designer negotiating a fee, and the lawyer not revealing any shock at what their client has done are all doing emotional labour as a routine and yet unpredictable part of their work. Feelings are managed in 'cold intimacy',[22] and are brought into economic activity through management psychologies like 'emotional intelligence'; they also precede and exceed economic activity. The feedback, ratings and reviews systems of platform apps become technological measurements of the apparent quality of emotional labour. Thinking about emotional labour reveals how the three ethical questions are interwoven. Work is organised in order to extract emotional labour, which draws out the interconnections of work and consumption or leisure, making up everyday life. Dignity becomes inherently contingent.

Collaborations and colleagues

Working on bodies or machines is one thing. But so much of doing work involves collaboration. Think about what it takes to run a restaurant. Restaurant workers need to know what their co-workers are doing if the service is to run smoothly. Work is a collective production, and so being a beginner, or being slow, or being tired, or being bossy affects work. Customers, chefs, waiters, cleaners, managers, cooked food, order technologies and ambience entwine. Looking at quite different contexts, a comparably complicated coordination of working bodies and technologies is also on show. Emergency service training involves working on coordination between colleagues, who learn to be aware of the environment in which they work, of the tools and machines they must use.[23] They learn to mirror each other, checking with their peripheral vision to see what colleagues are doing. The work is constantly changing and is not well understood if it is treated as a generalised abstraction –

'work' done by rational, independent, autonomous individuals. It's messier and more contingent, more specific and more relational than that implies. It's affected by how the work is managed, both by managerial and supervisory staff, and by the arrangements of tools, technologies and spaces, of course, but also by who and what else is in the space. That includes many kinds of negotiations around work. Former conflicts over how something should be done end up bedded in as the right way, or the way we do things round here. Coercive or manipulative negotiations have different resonances to negotiations that are open and collaborative and might or might not be repaired or concealed. Contingencies like being new, being trusted as 'a safe pair of hands', or being the kind of boss no one wants to help out are part of the everyday ethics and politics of doing work. Co-workers are both potential sources of working misery, for example, through bullying and mobbing, and of the assertion of dignity through supporting each other and fighting for improvements to working lives. Conviviality, the sense of what is right and the way co-workers know each other are important to people's sense of their work.

Dignity, infrastructures and bodies

How individual workers encounter the bodies of others, and what this constrains and enables, affects what work is like. Many discussions of work look at employment relationships or at work as a source of identity. But how work is done and what work does really matters to understanding the ethics and politics of work. Instead of taking the practice of work for granted, we should study it; instead of abstracting it as a question of 'low-, medium- and high-skilled work', we should think more precisely about what is involved. In the previous chapter, ideas about hidden and deleted work gave rise to an ethics of recognition. In this chapter, hidden work has been shown to also matter because of the ethical implications of thinking about how the world is shaped by work.

I do wonder why dignity is taken as the lodestar of ethics when it is so contradictory. It foregrounds the human and lays claim to universality. It finds dignity where there is autonomy.

It understands threats to dignity through managerial control and the design of work to limit autonomy, and in the conditions of work (the degree to which work is forced). But autonomy is based in a misreading of the relations between humans and with non-human entities, from winter weather to recalcitrant ink cartridges. Nature bites back, other humans intervene, machines, tools and other materials affect autonomy. Work exceeds managerial control even when work design may seek to embed control in the operations of machines.

The contradictions of dignity can be brought to light by thinking about infrastructures, work design and organisation. That ends the invisibility of some kinds of materialities that are central to doing work, but that are often taken for granted in studies of work. Doing this makes it possible to see the assemblages of work, the relations *between* colleagues, corporeality, technology and temporality. Through this, a different perspective on control emerges. Control appears as a complicated achievement not explainable as the outcome of dictates of managers made real. It extends beyond how working bodies act and into what they feel and what they do. Control is invisible, infrastructural and deleted.

Instead of foregrounding how work is controlled and managed, I am keen to make more of thinking about how work is done. So this story about technology is not simply one about managerial decisions. Instead it is about how technology design expertise assembles ways of working. In so doing, some activities are hidden (tacit knowledge that makes machines work), some are deleted (the new technology changes work), some are denied (eventually the design work itself becomes a mundane feature of infrastructure not worthy of notice), others are invisible (the emotional labour that work demands), and some are unanticipated because technologies do not obey the intentions of makers or decision-makers and delegate power in unintended ways. These uncertain effects come about because of negotiations between actors (not all of whom are human), as well as through domination.

FIVE

Work now

Introduction

Were you to ask a sociologist to describe the important features of the present right now, they might refer to the compression of time and space because of new communication technologies, a new interrogation of the value of human and non-human bodies because of biotech interference, and persistent, if shape-shifting and contested, social inequalities. The economic sociologist or political economist might add that global production and supply chains are more complex and denser than ever, and that a growing number of formerly non-market activities are increasingly marketised. Commentators on work are happy to make similar high-level claims about work as flexibilised, intensified and precarious. When unpaid work appears in these stories, it does so in relation to how it adds value to capitalism, as when private lives are captured by social media and generate economic value. Too few would think to say environmental crisis, and have a sense of how that affects these other phenomena. How could these phenomena be explained? So often, the answer is 'neoliberalism'.

Any story about the crises of present times has to confront the confused, overextended idea of neoliberalism. Like a poltergeist haunting policy, practice and the academic imaginary, neoliberalism seems always to be on hand, creating all kinds of strange and bad effects: outsourcing, work intensity, flexibilisation (to name but a few). In this chapter, I show that the historical realities to which the term is typically taken to refer are complex and uneven, relating to policy changes at the levels of supranational institutions, states, local institutions and corporations, and to economic and social ideas. It affects welfare provision, ownership, trade, tax and competition, and it affects how work is organised. It is as if it has captured all of social life, changing how people think and feel. But simple and sweeping statements about neoliberalism's power, its uniformity and its universalism underplay its wobbliness, and its critics might be guilty of contributing to its zombie powers. Understanding what's wrong with work now relies on recognising the interconnections between work and broad economic policy and practice, of course, and neoliberalism is an important but not comprehensive explanation for contemporary work practices, especially those that relate to flexibility and precariousness. The three questions about what's wrong with work come together in this chapter's focus on flexibility in work and precariousness in life. The challenge is to recognise the specificities of this moment in time without relying on over-extended explanations and simple abstractions, and so to distinguish between the ways in which work is exploitative and get appropriate insights into possibilities for change. The themes which I think really matter, technology, environment and informal work, will force their way into the discussion. Life now is a time of crisis, because of the precarious existence of human and non-human life, a precarity that has long existed in the majority world and is coming to the notice of the minority world, a precarity that affects all of life.

Neoliberalism: the key to all mythologies?

Neoliberalism is a – perhaps *the* – capitalocentric explanation that it captures all economic policy in its homogenising claws, and it seems also to capture all of life as it sets limits on how we think, feel and act. Neoliberalism refers to a set of economic ideas that assume that markets are the most effective way of allocating scarce resources and that they should be able to operate without interference. Other, that is, than those state-mandated regulations necessary to make that possible. If competition is the fundamental mechanism for fair allocations and for economic dynamism, then the state's role should be to guarantee competition between actors in any market, providing the fundamental legal protection against monopoly and in favour of competition. Western economic theory makes assumptions of methodological individualism (the idea that the behaviour of groups is best understood as an aggregate of the behaviour of individuals), that individuals are rational actors, and that the macroeconomic scale could and should mimic the 'perfect competition' of theories of microeconomic markets. Economic theory has implicitly normative ideas buried in its heart. If economic actors have voted with their purses and wallets to choose one outcome over another, then that outcome is economically efficient *and* socially desirable.

Beyond basic principles, it is hard to say clearly the extent to which 'neoliberalism' was and is a coherent intellectual movement. Mirowski and Plehwe[1] consider it a 'militant thought collective'. Economists rarely use the term.[2] Jamie Peck[3] says that there is no obvious 'origin' story for a neoliberal movement. Early meetings of the Mont Pelerin Society saw key neoliberal economists including Hayek, and scholars attached to the Chicago School, in dispute with each other. Neoliberal economists didn't agree with each other about neoliberal principles, about how to implement neoliberal policies, or about what the proper relationship between economic theory and messy politics should be. The essential contradictions of how to produce and maintain market rationality through the use of state power, without the state power overwhelming the market is not an easy one to sustain.

David Harvey's *A brief history of neoliberalism*[4] provides an account of the experiments with neoliberal policy-making. Chicago School neoliberal ideas were implemented in Chile by Pinochet's (US-backed) government, beginning in 1975. In Chile and elsewhere in South America, economic theory was shaped into economic policy. Public assets and natural 'resources' were privatised to end monopoly control by the state. That natural monopolies might not be amenable to competition was not really seen as a problem. Prioritising export-led growth and foreign direct investment changed the shape of economic activity; it brought changes to how work was organised and what was produced. It also shifted the boundaries of the nation-state as overseas companies gained local power, and as capital (and people) moved across borders, between sectors and regions. Chile was an experiment based on troubling hierarchical judgements by US policy-makers that it was okay to test policies on other countries first. It was neither the first nor the last time that market liberalism and political authoritarianism got friendly.

Neoliberal ideas appealed to technocrats, economists, bankers and policy-makers in global institutions, most importantly The World Bank from the 1970s. In part this was a response to the economic crisis of the times, made vivid in the stagflation, regulatory failures and structural changes of the 1970s. In the 1980s in the Global North, the UK and the US, the hotbeds of neoliberal macro policy-making brought in neoliberal reforms to money supply, to ownership of utilities, to taxation, and to the organisation of labour markets in the 1980s. Increased competition in labour markets relied on challenging the power of organised labour, and once trade unions had been made less powerful – fewer members and less cultural legitimacy – then reforms to labour law and norms were easier to put in place. Tax breaks were offered to corporations, as tax is inefficiency.

Already in these brief historical sketches, 'neoliberalism' involves a range of different processes and it involves an explicit politics. Being without clear origins and a manifesto make it adaptive, so that new crises tend to confirm the 'narrative' of neoliberal policy-making. In a catastrophe, and at the limits of knowledge, neoliberal policies appear to solve present problems. Every policy change is an experiment, and if it does not succeed, for example, if a new financial crisis lands, then it is because the experiment didn't go deep enough, there must be more marketisation, more competition. This is an ideology antagonistic to itself, mutating in response to its own limits.[5]

Seeing neoliberalisation as a variable set of practices, not a prescription, not a rigid policy agenda, is one step towards unpicking its apparent monolithic nature. Those practices often include promotion of export-oriented, financialised capital, preference for market-like governance and regulation, privatisation and – crucially for understanding work – opposition to social collectivities, denial of support for labour, and the redistribution of wealth to the already wealthy. The recognition of variable practices means that it is possible to see that neoliberal economic policy is unevenly applied to territories and scales (and may not be the only policy game in town), as practices meet history, institutions and other specificities. Once again in this discussion, the long histories of colonialism and uneven economic development are important in affecting 'variegated neoliberalism',[6] as are national understandings of economic ideas.[7] How might that be done?

Expertise assembles

Neoliberalism – like other economic practices – is made, not given. It is made through expert work (bearing in mind that 'work' always includes an encounter between humans and other human and non-human objects) located in specific relation to a range of technologies and to the power to enact change. That is, expertise is not merely the property of individuals, but is in assemblages. This is a way of thinking about how politics is done, and about how technocratic ethics operates. Ethical claims are used to rationalise decisions and normalise policies. Neoliberal policy is made in the design of spreadsheets, the glass-sided corridors of Big Four accounting firms, in the backscratching groupthink of MBA-trained 'elites'. It is made by nation-states and global agencies, and by the actions of corporations. Some kinds of knowledge count, and are used to work out policy solutions that suit national settings. To put it another way, 'neoliberal practices do not merely encounter, and then "carve through", pre-existing and inert institutional landscapes; rather, they are actively and combatively fashioned in order to transform targeted features of these landscapes'.[8]

Studies of how economic policies are brought in, in what sense they are or are not neoliberal and how they vary between places are essential to an understanding of how economies are made.

The spread and mutability of neoliberal ideas is influenced by how a particular version of economics has dominated policies in states, global agencies and corporations. It is not the only way of doing economics, but it is dominant. Learning economics seems like a technological training, even training in science.

It is also full of a hidden curriculum of values that deny being values: that efficiency is socially desirable, for example. As discussed in Chapter One, processes of economisation are not neutral, and how economic expertise assembles knowledge and translates it into 'how it should be done' is a critical element of the power of technocratic operations that enact neoliberal policies. A combination of a rather homogeneous economics profession, the standardised tools and techniques of economics, and the training of political elites in economic thinking has injected specific versions of economic knowledge – based in US liberalism – into the heart of nation-states, politics and civil services.[9] International students doing US economics degrees in the US and the Nobel economics prize are two examples of how economic ideas are translated as global truths. Intellectual, policy and practitioner networks enabled neoliberal ideas to reach around the globe.[10] However, there is no such thing as an entirely homogeneous academic discipline with equivalent effects everywhere. Disagreements between neoliberal economic thought, different policy settings and different ideologies, different institutions and different ways of making policy agreements make for different outcomes. Nonetheless, there are some drivers towards homogeneity.

Global agencies

Of the many and varied global and regional institutions that affect how work is organised (the EU, ASEAN, the IMF), it is The World Bank that has had the most far-reaching impact on work, and that is key to the global expansion of neoliberal policy. The World Bank is a financing agency. How and what it finances has an effect on employment that it has only acknowledged in the last 10 years. It has done little until this year to implement its own recently developed guidance on meeting core labour standards, despite years of pressure from the ITUC and ILO. It has promoted structural adjustments to national economies to reduce the costs of 'doing business' – the title of its annual report on business regulations in different places intended to help corporations decide where to locate and how to operate. *Doing business* has long made for pretty grim reading, especially for the 'employing workers indicator' (EWI). For many years the EWI scored best in places where minimum wages were lowest, where hours of work were longest and where paid workers had fewest protections. The EWI was used as part of the evidence for assessing whether a country qualified for a World Bank loan, and its effects will be seen in the subsequent discussions of flexibility and precarity. If the conditions for getting a World Bank loan were deregulating labour markets, well, that was a price many nation-states have thought worth paying.

From 2018, World Bank projects are supposed to comply with labour standards and to consider the effects of projects on jobs. Its (draft) World Development Report 2019, entitled *The changing nature of work*, addresses the future of work. The sharp irony of using a painting by Mexican communist artist Diego Rivera as the cover[11] seems lost. Recognising both changes to how work is commonly organised, as well as how traditional work-based safety nets do not suit the flexible work to which the Bank has contributed, it suggests that reviving and remaking social assistance programmes (via nation-states) is key. Better social assistance sounds great, but hold on a moment. The report hopes that will enable more labour flexibilisation. After all, minimum wages aren't so necessary if there is social assistance. Reading the discussion below will give you a sense of whether you think there has been enough flexibilisation already.

When even economists are wary of flexibilisation, it might be time to slow down. The snappily titled 'The imprudence of labour market flexibilization in a fiscally austere world' is a paper critical of policy-makers 'pressed by their country's circumstances or their own political beliefs'[12] who argued for labour market flexibilisation and reductions in public sector work on top of fiscal austerity. Downwards pressure on wages might boost financial markets in the short term, but it reduces consumption in the medium and long term. What role, then, do nation-states play?

Nation-states

Variations in economic ideologies and practices are clearly present,[13] and these variations might be acknowledged as well as similarities.[14] National and local political projects are hybrids, not simply 'neoliberal'. Creative industry policy is a good example for this, exhibiting, on the one hand, a 'neoliberal' entrepreneurial, problem-solving strategy for a knowledge economy, and on the other hand, often doing so at the insistence of economic nationalism in the face of global competition.[15]

Aihwa Ong[16] disputes the assumption that neoliberalism is an all-consuming power and makes much of the multiplicities and differences of geography and history. In her investigations of South-East Asian states, she finds neoliberalism brought in as an exception to authoritarian, post-socialist and post-colonial states. That is to say, these are not 'neoliberal states', but states that use neoliberal policies as exceptions, in order to do specific things, say, to generate growth through special economic zones (SEZs) and export processing zones (especially common in China – perhaps the most obvious instance of a state that is not neoliberal but that uses neoliberal policies). SEZs are regions with different kinds of tax regimes, different forms of subsidy and with different labour laws to the rest of the nation. Space is managed, and within it, populations are controlled, workforces are made and moralised – maybe in contradictory ways (as economically productive, which is good, as women with perhaps too much freedom from traditional controls, which is bad). In addition to neoliberalism as an exceptional policy (and hence not a dominant way of being, thinking and feeling), there are the exceptions to neoliberalism, in this instance, populations who might be protected from damaging effects of neoliberalism, or in/excluded from citizenship.

Policies and practices labelled neoliberal (for example, SEZs where tax and labour regulations are weighted in favour of the interests of global corporations) have a clear effect on how work is organised. However, describing the changes to work only in relation to neoliberalism tells a partial story. The common claims on display in the literature on work too often make (implicit) neocolonial assumptions that things that matter in the UK and US, where neoliberal policies and practices are strong, will inevitably and in the same kind of way be extended elsewhere. This is an extension of 'stages of development' hierarchies (discussed in Chapter Two) that assume some places are leaders and others will catch up, and that the modes of living and structures of feeling that exist in the US will emerge elsewhere in time. Economy-first explanations make impossible the idea that hierarchy drives economy, instead seeing inequalities as the result of economic practice. But instead of the quick explanation of 'it's all neoliberal', it is worth thinking about how processes and practices that fit with specific elements of neoliberal ideas exist in combination within economic–nationalist agendas (as in, say, Malaysia), or with neoconservative social policies (as with austerity in Britain), or with other intervening and mediating entities. Otherwise homogenising stories are told, simple stories, misrepresentative stories.

Corporate management

Management is formalised and credentialised through higher education qualifications, especially MBAs. The curriculum they learn promotes profit maximising as desirable, and assumes that in other ways economic activity and the quest for profit is value neutral.[17] Such assumptions affect how work gets organised. Indeed, it is through such assumptions that the 'business case' for forced labour is made as ethically okay, against alternative ethics that might argue such reasoning is unthinkable. MBAs teach norms of how management should act, and management consultancies spread standard audit, governance and analysis strategies, and these elements of a global business culture act as the Trojan horse of profit maximisation. Through such practices, theories of flexibility become ordinary experience, managed and made through technologies. Expert communities are thereby important and powerful. Technical expertise that does not appear to be political is privileged: it's hard to argue with apparently neutral, apparently scientific claims – and indeed neoliberal policies tend to rely on standardisation to justify claims, demonstrate reputation and rationalise competition.[18] So 'economic science' or 'management science' creates practices and outcomes that appear to be good, no matter what the broader consequences, and that are defended by 'professional ethics'.

Even economic activities by corporations are, however, not understandable solely as the ever-deepening effects of the neoliberal ethos. Corporations are complex entities, constituted through their activities. They are not simply detached agents, separated from states, actively pursuing profit through globalisation and benefiting from neoliberal state policies. Contestation between social groups within corporations, including corporate managers, financiers, shareholders, suppliers and labour, show that outcomes are not given, or fixed for all time.[19] Some corporations are firmly rooted within nations, others are footloose organisations with extended supply chains. Some are asset-stripping global conglomerations with bizarre portmanteau names, others are slow-growing, have worker training programmes or place stress on maintaining reputation, longevity and status. Refusing to see the differences and consider the implications for work and life makes for a restricted understanding of what corporations do in the world.

The new way of the world?

Commentators on contemporary life and on work often use neoliberalism as *the* explanation for present work arrangements. Dardot and Laval consider the 'new way of the world' as an intensely neoliberal society that gives rise to a 'new human condition' marked by constant competition.[20] It's very easy to give an account that is clear and coherent, retrofitting the designation 'neoliberal' to flatten differences, and to give the impression that early experiments spread elsewhere to generate a wholeheartedly neoliberal present. That kind of two-dimensional history makes it easy to make claims about the omnipresence of neoliberalism as the best explanation for the trends in the organisation of work – that selves are captured by work, for example, or that neoliberalism produces precarity. 'Neoliberalism everywhere' sounds just like the explanations given 10 years earlier for US-dominated globalisation – and that turned out to be too blunt a claim.[21] If you start with the US when you think about global patterns and interdependencies, then perhaps 'neoliberalism everywhere' is a reasonable view. But political and economic power is more diffuse and its organisation more complex than that implies. In the history of apparently neoliberal times, the more differentiated story about macroeconomic policy and its effects gives nuance to understanding the variability of contemporary work.

I am a bit suspicious of making a move from macro policy to the experience of work. If neoliberal policy has not mapped out an apparently singular linked and co-dependent territory, then how can it explain the variations in how work is organised and interconnected, and in what it does? So the quick'n'easy explanation 'it's because of neoliberalism' doesn't explain enough about 'what's wrong with work'. There can be a double misrecognition, when all economic processes are misrecognised as neoliberal, and when all processes are recognised as economic (for example, conflating the neoconservative social agenda of the US with neoliberal economics). How to disentangle what is entangled in these kinds of explanations? What effect do neoliberalism's mutations and its outsides have?

In the next section, my aim is not to assess the extent to which 'neoliberalism' does and doesn't explain contemporary work. It is to suggest that saying 'it's neoliberalism' doesn't generate enough understanding of the complex global organisation of work. It is to talk through flexibility and precariousness as inflected by neoliberalism and its alloys and alliances, while recognising that one-word abstractions are not enough. This involves bearing in mind the arguments made by economic geographers about multiplicity and the uneven nature of that neoliberal imposition and noting the observation of Harris and Scully that 'the inordinate scholarly and popular focus on the ills of neoliberalism over the past 30 years has produced a major confusion about the causes of precarity in contemporary life'.[22]

Twenty-first century work

Paid work is affected by the mantra of flexibility. But so, too, is unpaid work and the whole of the rest of life. Flexible production, Just-in-time, lean production and outsourcing in global production networks (as discussed in Chapter Two) are production strategies that rely on labour flexibility. They require particular forms of work organisation, rely on and create interconnections between work, and have different effects in the world to other ways of organising work. In turn, these production strategies are affected by state institutions and corporations, by available technologies and infrastructures, by human and non-human 'inputs'. Flexibility gives paid work in the present a triple vulnerability: vulnerability to the time of work, to access to work and to what work will work demand. I'll pay attention to time flexibility and work intensity here in order to develop a further understanding of 'work-related insecurities'[23] that emerge from a world in which labour market informality and precarity are common. Adding temporal flexibility to the problems with work identified in previous chapters suggests a world of misery and pain. On the face of it, the story about work time is essentially one where Question 1, the organisation of work, is central. Answering only that question, however, would produce a flattened account. So it's important to remember Question 2, about modes of interconnection between work, and Question 3, about how work produces realities.

Time flexibility

Factory work on Fordist production lines has often been taken as the exemplar for work against which other work compares (see Chapter Two). Factory work brings a particular politics of time: struggles over the length of the working day and over the quantity of work expected in a working day, where the production line shouldn't stop, where the god of productivity demands the 'Human Motor' work like a machine,[24] and where time and motion studies vary as to whether they accept that workers' bodies get tired. Time discipline is fundamental to industrial work, but the politics of time has a different resonance now.

Life has polyphonic rhythms that exceed linear, chronological, factory clock time. The politics and ethics of work time now reflects a polyphonic idea of time more than a linear one. Time flexibility in production demands and relies on flexibility in life. This means an always-on workforce that is forced to subsume their bodily needs to managerial edicts as to how long a toilet break can be, and that practices a choreography of care to juggle family life, employment and other work. There is no escape into sleep when technologies extend the working day for some workers, who check emails on their mobiles from bed.[25] The stressed-out knowledge worker, overwhelmed with work that cannot be done in the time and space available by the body that is supposed to do it, facing deadlines and demanding customers, finds little merit in time flexibility.

It's worth noting that there are notable differences in national norms about working hours among otherwise similar privileged workers.[26] And while the 'stressed-out executive' who regularly travels across time zones or puts in 70-hour weeks in a macho presentee-ist corporation might seem like the poster boy of long working hours, his is only one version of stress through overwork, and he is able to rely on paid and unpaid personal services to keep the show on the road: the cooks and waiters, cleaners and carers, taking early morning or late night buses to low-paid jobs that keep knowledge workers going. Long hours, unpredictable hours and anti-social hours are part of contemporary working lives, either explicitly mandated by employers, or self-imposed by workers who've learned to identify deeply with their organisation or profession. Long working hours are not new features of low-skilled and low-paid work, and the exhaustion that creates the conditions for emotional despair and suicidal thoughts such as those at Orange in France or Foxconn in China is not new either.

Agency work

Beginning in the 1950s, and promoted more extensively in the 1960s, temp agencies in the US offered 'the semi-permanent employee', already trained in secretarial skills, and eligible for few of the expensive benefits of regular workers. Global expansion followed later. This is gig work, before the term became common. Temps are now used in countries in the Global North to provide staff for manufacturing and transport, more than for administration.[27] In part, this is because admin work is now done differently, via email and individual computers, and in part it's because of the flexibilisation of these other sectors. Agency workers, or 'dispatched workers', as they are referred to in East Asia,[28] are hired by agencies and sent out to other companies. That means that temp agencies are important mediators. Numbers of temp workers are increasing: in the UK, from 50,000 in the mid-1980s to 270,000 in the mid-2000s (still less than one-tenth of the labour force); in China there are estimated to be 60 million, a fifth of the labour force.[29] Globalised temp agencies like Adecco and Manpower are active players in flexibilisation. The appeal to firms is offering numerical flexibility; to workers it is enabling them to meet other demands.

The use of temp agencies is one instance where local labour laws affect the status of nominally comparable workers. In the UK, agency workers are not considered employees but in most other places they are. Sometimes the agency is considered to be the employer (in East Asia and most of Europe); in others the firm where they actually do work is the employer (in Canada and sometimes in the US).[30] How the employment relationship is configured affects what the work is like. Confused regulations or unclear lines of responsibility or unequal treatment means that agency workers may do similar work to formally employed staff, but without benefits. Where there are regulations, these can be circumvented. In Japan, where regulations say that an agency worker assigned to the same job for three years should be offered regular employment status after this time, it's common to change their job title or move them to another branch.[31] Elsewhere, 'payrolling' turns permanent workers into temps, while they do the same jobs. Whole sectors of a firm might have the same principle applied (cleaning services in hotels have used this a lot).

The trend towards the greater use of temporary and agency workers takes different forms in different places, and there are also enormous differences within the category of 'temp' worker. In one US warehouse, Beth Gutelius[32] identified five categories of worker, four of whom do very similar jobs but under different contracts and with different experiences of contingency. With only managers directly employed by the logistics firm she studied, three kinds of outsourced workers came from one outsourced agency: 'team leaders', 'permatemps' with a feeling of permanency if not the rights of a permanent employee, and 'seasonals' with two- or three-month contracts. Another temp agency was used to provide 'supertemps', those employed daily or hourly to fill in gaps. Pay, rights and benefits matched the hierarchy of employment.

Contracts

Along with the decline in the 'job for life' (which was only ever a job for life for some) came a changing story about work. A job for life sounds boring in relation to the alternatives of 'portfolio careers' and so on. Contemporary work is marked not only by this instability, re-positioned as desirable for a modern worker craving self-expression and reinvention, but by shorter-term instabilities. Once it was easy to speak about 'standard' employment contracts (full-time wage or salary work), and it was possible to get away without acknowledging that those 'standard' contracts were more likely to be available to male workers in developed economies working in credentialised occupations. Standard employment refers to stereotypical ideas about a permanent job, carried out in set hours (9–5), with holiday entitlement. 'Standard' could be compared to a varied range of 'non-standard' employment, which included all kinds of part-time contracts. It is now rarer to see those 'standard' contracts. Part-time work is more common, not only for women with children, but for many other workers too, and 'flexible working' is more extensive. 'Non-standard' is widely variable, including a range of contracts, and differing according to the local/regional/national labour markets, and according to state regulations on labour contracts.

The prevalence and ordinariness of part-time employment, legal, cultural and statistical differences in what constitutes a 'standard' and the dependencies between kinds of work all make the idea of 'standard' complicated. What does standard look like for the female informatics workers doing data processing in Barbados?[33] They work a triple shift: standard paid work, domestic work and informal economic activities such as selling cakes. What about the social services staff on insecure contracts who donate labour, in the form of unpaid overtime, in order to keep their jobs?[34] That is 'standard' work that expects extra volunteering from the worker. It's better, I think to avoid claiming something is or is not standard, stressing instead how normal are independent contractors, day labourers, temporary workers, seasonal workers, on-call workers, sub-subcontracted workers; those on fixed-term contracts, zero hours contracts; those without contracts but with long-term relationships in a workplace.

Time flexibility bites hardest for those employed on zero hours contracts or other kinds of forced flexibility. Flexibilisation, justified through the privileging of the immediate 'needs of the business', means that workers are not guaranteed working hours and so are not guaranteed pay. They might not work during quiet periods of the day, week or year. Compared to an open-ended, gold-standard employment contract with statutory protection against dismissal, other contracts – zero hours, fixed-term, contingent – generate precariousness. On their own, these kinds of fragile contracts have bad effects. The effects are worsened when life is not buttressed by any kind of social support if and when the next contract doesn't appear. It adds up to vulnerability and misery.

Precarious lives

The prevalence of contingent work contracts and time flexibility are key to descriptions of contemporary work as precarious. Definitions of precariousness vary. Hardt and Negri are deliberately ambiguous in framing precarity as 'temporal poverty'.[35] For Herod and Lambert,[36] precarity has four elements: low earnings, minimal social safety net, little regulatory protection and limited autonomy in shaping work. These elements combine to damage people's lives. When hours are long and work time is unpredictable, it's hard to plan from day to day – and it's very tiring. It's hard to think about a future when you don't know how long you'll have your job. The content of precarious jobs might in themselves be damaging to workers, but the long hours and stress make them even unhealthier. The possibility of moving is high, but the possibility of moving to something better is low. Getting training, getting transferable skills, is hard, in part because paid work is a one-sided commitment, with employers having considerably more control than workers on how work gets done and how it is rewarded. That, plus few regulations and rights, makes workers vulnerable.

The elements of precarity combine to make for different kinds of precariousness.[37] Precariousness in employment means objective job insecurity; precarious work refers to 'non-standard jobs'; precarious workers are those who cannot live well now or plan for the future; the precariat is a class of insecure workers; and precarity per se is the social conditions that come from living in environments dominated by insecurity even for those who do not have precarious work – so when a group of workers with comparatively good pay and conditions negotiate on the basis of a fear that they, too, might become precarious, then they live in precarity. These distinctions delineate the different kinds of encounters with precarity that certain kinds of workers might experience. For example, students who have precarious jobs are often not precarious workers, when family supports them, or training for different careers, although in their early experience of work they learn about working in a precarious setting. To put it another way, the social relations of work and life matter, and can 'amplify' or 'cushion'[38] the experience of work, and not all precarious work creates a precarious worker. There is not a standard way of 'living under neoliberalism'. The adverse incorporation of unfree workers into global production networks experience a precarious existence qualitatively different to the student temporarily in a precarious job. In Lee and Kofman's words, 'in the global south, precariousness at work creates not just a crisis of job quality at the point of production but also a crisis of social reproduction'.[39] Unstable work, unprotected work – of the kind engendered by World Bank programmes – makes for precarious, vulnerable lives.

In the US, the uneven effects of precarious work are commonly related to increased polarisation between good and bad jobs.[40] Job polarisation means a decline in middle-range employment, but an increase in both high-status/skilled work and low-status/skilled work, and in relation to rewards for work that are increasingly unequal between groups and between individuals. Kalleberg, the author of the study, says that these twin elements emerge from neoliberal changes, including globalisation, technologies, deregulation, macroeconomic policy that focused on low inflation/price stability and not full employment. This means that low wages, high unemployment, debt-fuelled growth, the importance given to shareholder interests not worker interests and declining union power all contributed to firms choosing more flexible employment relations. The US case doesn't generalise elsewhere, though. For example, the relationship between precarious and non/less precarious work is variable. Part-time and temporary workers are more common where standard workers have decent job protection, and are used to produce flexibility.[41] Sometimes (often in the Global South, and in the UK), informal work is used as a selection filter for permanent or formal work.

While political consent for labour market flexibilisation often positions nation-states as passive in the face of unprecedented forces (those powerful economic and technological beasts again), this erases how states get involved in creating the conditions to which they only pretend to respond. For example, China has generated a precarious workforce as part of its strategy of development,[42] in particular, as a way of creating a large workforce for the new manufacturing cities out of rural migration, with those in rural regions willing to travel because of the effect of earlier policies that first encouraged and then retracted credit provision. Migrants to urban regions are entitled only to temporary work permits and keep their rural registrations. This affects how they can access healthcare, pensions and so on when away from their region of birth.[43] Decisions by the Chinese state affect those of neighbours, as do other decision-marking institutions. The Asia Development Bank, for example, has been important in positioning the Greater Mekong region as an SEZ, fully connected to global value chains, gated and controlled to limit worker rights. It has done this by agricultural modernisation programmes that generate new surplus workers, for example.

Experiences in the Global North of flexibilisation and precarity caused by neoliberal practices cannot be applied straightforwardly to the Global South. State development policies and strategies of capital accumulation predate neoliberal programmes,[44] when it was thought that commodification and formalisation would be a pathway to development. That wasn't true. Indeed, the social assistance programmes (for example, cash transfers to the poorest people) used by some Global South states (quite distinct from the welfare states of the Global North) reduce the extent to which citizens depend on commodified paid labour.

Precarious work affects the emotional lives of workers and their physical security. It assaults not just working lives, but the whole of life. Long working hours might also squeeze out the space for domestic work, or cause minor crises in family care arrangements. Stress and anxiety in work contribute also to the unpaid work of caring for family and friends. The stress of an excess of work is significant and the stress of not enough paid work is also significant. Neither is desirable. Neither are solely the effects of 'neoliberalism'. Insurgent nature, unpredictable human relationships and technological breakdowns contribute to precarious work and precarious life in ways that exceed the economic explanation of 'neoliberalism', tempting though that explanation is. Further, neither economic policies nor processes are simply 'neoliberal'. The challenge of understanding how people live in the present and what their work is like can't yet be met.

End of Part One:
Everyday life, technology and environment in the present

I mentioned earlier that 'neoliberalism' provides a strong but overwrought explanation for the organisation of contemporary work as flexible and as precarious. In Part One of the book, I have shown that economic explanations tend to dominate questions about work. They are persuasive, but they are always partial. All-powerful but nebulous forces such as 'neoliberalisation' (see also globalisation, technology and economy – the four horsemen of the infernal alternative) need more delineation, especially when applied to explaining precarious lives. Familiar arguments return again: what kinds of work are being considered in claims to increased precarity, what complexities are being downplayed in the sweeping claims of a new world of work? Paid work has always had precarious elements if you look beyond the labour aristocracy of unionised (male) manufacturing in countries with decent welfare state settlements. Day labouring has long been common in construction; agricultural work relies on desperate seasonal workers; domestic service workers are vulnerable to being dismissed (without employer references) if they don't show respect or respectability. So in the glorious days of full employment and good working lives, there were many without protection, both those in and outside of formal employment. Misrecognition demands re-description and re-evaluation, so that variegations, exceptions and silent currents might be noticed. These redescriptions might be emotionally and pragmatically important for finding alternatives to exploitative work.

Despite all the talk of marketisation and commodification, there are outsides to neoliberalism. A small story from Dimitris Dalakoglou[1] gives one example. New roads funded by the EU were built in post-socialist Albania. Albanian people work at building and maintaining the roads, and drive the cars and lorries that carry through the goods and people that show how much Albania has changed, and which marks its singular position in the global economy. Economic change and new work stems from these open borders. It's recognisably Albania, but it's also recognisably changed. This deregulation connects the actions of the state, the work lives and debts of Albanian citizens, and the production and consumption of goods and services in Albania and elsewhere. Neoliberally informed deregulation is the simple explanation, but it misses what Dalakoglou finds: that people just use the roads *because they now can* when they couldn't before. They like doing it. They do it for sensory, aesthetic, political and cultural reasons. Everyday life is not reducible to economic explanations.

Despite the similarities between techno-rationality and econo-rationality, technological change is not identical to economic change, it is not simply the outcome of capitalistic urges. It is easy to assume that neoliberal capitalism and technology are part and parcel of the same system, so reliant on IT are the standards and accountability mechanisms of neoliberal technocracy, and so in keeping with each other at the level of discourse. Think of the 'California Ideology'[2] of seamless, friction-free capitalism. Here is the techno-libertarian world where fibre optic cables permit the free flow of information (so essential to the neoliberal assumptions about how markets work) at supersonic speed. That means that software can send information back to the post-Fordist factory *just in time*; where error-prone human interventions get managed out. Here's the dream of markets free of state intervention and made possible by tech. This 'machinic globality'[3] is a fantasy of a borderless market without imperfection. Believing in the promises of tech companies to create a friction-free technological infrastructure is risky stuff (Chapter Four hints at what is deleted, Chapter Seven will take that further). To me, though, this kind of high-tech world is a co-conspirator with, not a product of, neoliberal action. They may share assumptions about human agents and the power of rational actors. To reduce IT to a story of neoliberalism is to make it impossible to understand its own workings.

Collapsing 'nature' – complex, heterogeneous, multiple – into the ways it is exploited by capitalist accumulation in general and neoliberalism in particular is as reductive. Nature exceeds the 'resource' view of it, and has its own very powerful insurgent effects. And it encounters neoliberal ideas (in all their variegation) in many ways. Carbon trading or wetlands banking are solutions that emerge from the melding of ecological troubles and neoliberal solutionism through marketisation – but that is not the same as privatisation of natural resources or regulation of the extraction of precious metals. What's going on, how's it organised, and what work is involved are not the same.[4] What is more important here is that when the refrain 'What about the environment?' starts tapping away again, any discussion of precarity also changes. Precarity stops being the property of an individual or class's relationship to the labour market. It becomes instead a question of how existence is precarious: to farm in an area prone to flooding, or to make a career from protecting a vulnerable natural world that is threatened by economic development is to have a different engagement with the world, and to think differently about what work does in the world. This precarious nature is not a simple outcome of neoliberal processes. And a number of tensions appear: pickers who extract precious metals from discarded consumer waste do work that is 'green' but it is scarcely decent: dirty, dangerous and unpleasant, as well as poorly paid. What happens here is that by engaging and responding to the precarity of the earth in such work, some kinds of workers face damage to their own lives.

Everyday life, technology and environment are all central to understanding what's wrong with work now. In Part Two, I focus on each, asking what does looking in detail at these knots tell us about how work is organised, how kinds of work are interconnected and what work does, in order to see how these quintessential problems of the present contribute to understanding what's wrong with work.

Part Two

SIX

Informal work and everyday life

Introduction

Informal work preceded neoliberalism, and it exceeds capitalism. A snapshot of informal work research reveals subsistence activities such as street vending in many cities,[1] cash-in-hand babysitting for neighbours in the UK,[2] a complex economy of favours and non-market exchanges in Russia,[3] and a whole host of other hardly visible, ordinary work activities. Estimates of the prevalence of informal work vary; the ILO has recently suggested 60 per cent of employed people work in the informal economy.[4] In the first of three chapters that explore the specific knots that mark present times as especially challenging (see Chapter One), this chapter looks in detail at informal work as part of how everyday life is lived. I suggest in this chapter that what's wrong with work can't be understood without acknowledging the mesh/mess of work and life together, and that a focus on informal work is essential to seeing that.

Informal activity, however, often has the condition of 'non-existence',[5] being residual, inferior, local and non-productive. Recognition, not deletion, has to be a starting point for considering the ethical issues of work. Informal work includes wage labour without employment contracts or regulation, and small-scale self-employment; it might be done simultaneously with childcare, as in the case of homeworkers subcontracted to do piecework for electronics manufacturers, and it might be childcare. By studying the many different forms of informal work and informal economic activity and how they make livelihoods, it's possible to understand much more about how different kinds of work are connected, including how formally contracted work relates to the informal (as when people learn to sew at home in order to get informal paid work in satellite factories).

In this chapter, I'll look in more detail at the complexity and variety of informal work, how it relates to global inequalities, how it contributes to, but is not reducible to, capitalist exchange and can only be partly understood in the language of an all-enveloping neoliberalism. In thinking about informal work, I hear echoes in the discussions of precarious work, as well as in the gig economy, and domestic work: different but overlapping forms of work. Attending to their similarities and differences contributes to thinking about a better future. Taken together, these elements are reminders of the arguments I made in Chapter Three about the relationship between work and life. A focus on informal work points out the many different ways in which work can be organised, the complexity of the interconnections between kinds of work on both global and intimate levels, as well as the very important way that work makes survival possible – and bad work makes survival so hard.

Informal is normal

If you've ever spilled those bits of polystyrene used in packaging and tried to pick them up, then you'll have some sense of what it's like trying to tie down what 'informal work' means. Just when you think you've got it all covered, there's another dimension, another thing to pick up. That's one of the reasons why informal work is such an important knot to worry at when making sense of what's wrong with work. It is varied and extensive, and it is thoroughly present – even if, as was discussed in Chapters Two and Three, it can tend to be hidden and misrecognised. Given the great variety of informal work, the first topic to address is what is gained by talking about 'the informal sector' or 'informal work'. Those phrases do tend to generate a sense that there is a definable, bounded notion of the formal against which the informal can be compared. Actually applying that definition is hard, though: connections take many forms and vary in time and space, and the interdependencies between formal and informal work complicate answers to my questions about 'What's wrong with work?' Work that is not a job, with a contract, with a plan for the future, but a way of getting by right now can't be imagined as having the same politics as those formalised factory jobs. Further, thinking about the idea that work – as the activities necessary for the maintenance of life – can't be dealt with by packing it up in a little box marked 'reproduction' or 'household', then the possible range of ethical and political responses to the problem with work are very different. The very diversity and extensiveness of informal work makes it all the more important to consider, to hold it up to the light and really question it.

Informalisation affected countries with high and low levels of economic development; it affected a range of sectors, including agriculture, manufacturing, care and services,[6] but of course its effects vary. Scholars and policy-makers trying to understand informal work have worked hard to find adequate definitions that acknowledge and accept that it is highly differentiated, and that make it possible to measure those informal activities that are hidden from view (either spatially hidden, that is, it is done in private, or conceptually hidden, by not being counted as work). The ILO has been commissioning research into the informal sector since the 1970s. Researchers worked initially with a fairly rigid binary between the formal and informal sectors. They considered informal low-wage and low-skilled workers to be a residual group, not yet absorbed by the formal sector. They thought that economic development would get rid of informal work, that which has no employment contract and which is not regulated. That didn't happen. Where discussions about informal economic activity see it as a stage on the way to more desirable formalisation – as immature, as undesirable excess, or as a residue – then they engage in capitalocentrism, making the assumption that progress is measured by the capture of life in a system of profit extraction through wage labour. It's worth noting that governments might quite like formalisation as a way to increase tax revenue, if not to provide regulated work.

The earlier theorisation considers informal sectors as those where state regulations are absent (economic activity that is not registered, regulated or taxed). More recent explanations of persistent informality often now stress globalisation and neoliberal labour market policies that weakened the links between workers and formal employers and institutions.[7] Structural adjustment programmes (privatisation, budget cuts) to reduce the size of the state, and ideological support for global competition and foreign investment both contributed to the explosion of informal work. Rather than absence of regulation, nation-states and para-state institutions such as The World Bank are all-too present when macroeconomic policies involve being 'export-oriented'. This contributes to an amorphous labour force, hidden and informal, that is used flexibly to meet labour demand, but whose ability to live well doesn't seem to matter when the need for their flexible work disappears. Women may often be especially flexible in this way, and family and care work changes as paid work changes. However, grand abstractions are easily overstated and don't always best reflect the historical specificity of what they are called on to explain. Informal work pre-dates World Bank neoliberal policies in the Global South, so that it is both historically wrong to explain informalisation like that, and draws attention to some parts of the informal economy (outsourced workers, discussed in the section entitled 'Both home and work' below), while ignoring that which is not so obviously connected to global production networks.[8]

Making more precise distinctions between strata of informal work is essential.[9] Some informal activities are part of an institutionalised relationship between formal and informal work, for example, when transnational companies with global supply chains rely on outsourced informal productive labour, and when states allow that. Informal workers here are victims in relation to the power of capital – a dependent exploitation. Informalisation comes from above. That is quite different from informal work that provides the microentrepreneurs with some ability to respond to situations, and lower costs where they don't pay tax. That might help them to accumulate the necessary capital to grow. That differs again from survival and subsistence activities, which, in the case of street children in Accra, involves a lot of waiting around and cooperating with friends in order to get bits of work.[10] The strata are not mutually exclusive in practice. The division between formal and informal work is often blurred, and people might do both kinds of work. Those doing informal work might move frequently between different kinds of (formal and informal) work, or they might have a longstanding, if complex, arrangement of kinds of work. They may be affected by their citizenship status, as some are temporary migrants within and between country borders, and others do informal work precisely because they cannot or do not want to move to places where formal jobs could be available.[11] Informal activities are interconnected with formal activities. These interconnections are spatial (in global, regional and local terms), temporal (especially in relation to households) and sectoral (for example, across a supply chain informal and formal economic organisation appears in different moments). Informal activities differ also in how exploitative they are. Unfree labour and adverse incorporation certainly happen in the sector.

Good hard data

The ILO has a mandate to find a way of measuring the range of informal activity. It considers informal employment to happen in formal and informal economic sectors, and differentiates between the type of production unit (formal, informal, household) and the form of employment (formal or informal), and it measures all these things. The statistical evidence, however, has to be treated cautiously. In part that's because 'good hard data' is hard to come by, but as soon as data gets put into a table, it takes on a life of its own, no matter how much the author admits 'but of course it's more complicated than that'. The lines between rows and columns create such an aura of certainty and imply that objective truths have been identified. The other problem is that the data available cannot be trusted because of the complexities of measuring informality. Indeed, in recognition of this, ILO researchers seem to write as much about measurement problems in the informal economy as they do about the results of those attempts at measurement. Any analysis is constrained by how informal work is hidden, and is not measured in comparable ways in different places. That definitions change, data is absent or partial, and measurement attempts thereby limited, has some other consequences. If the real extent of informal work isn't really known, then it is easier to ignore or sideline the challenges it makes to, say, World Bank flexibilisation policies which prefer the higher productivity of flexibilised formal workers.

A few features of the data I present are worth noting. The data was gathered in different years, and using different methodologies. Some of it is estimated. Data is gathered at nation-state level, although there are inevitably enormous differences within nation-states (and groups of workers who might be even less visible than most informal workers). Most of the data excludes agricultural workers. That's because including agricultural work can risk making changes to non-agricultural work invisible (where 90 per cent of the population work in agriculture, as in some parts South-East Asia and sub-Saharan Africa, then shifts in the proportion of non-agricultural informal work could hardly be spotted). Finally, data on the Global North is dealt with separately to other data, as it is by the ILO.

Table 6.1 shows that non-agricultural informal employment is well over half of all employment in most regions. It seems to have grown in North Africa, Latin America, Southern and South-East Asia and in the post-socialist transition countries. In sub-Saharan Africa it has gone up, but it is not as high as

Table 6.1: Employment in the informal economy as a percentage of non-agricultural employment by five-year periods in various regions and sub-regions

	1975-79	1980-84	1985-89	1990-94	1995-99	2000-04	2005-10
Northern Africa	39.6		34.1		47.5	47.3	53
Sub-Saharan Africa		*67.3*	*72.5*	76.0	*86.9*	*63.3*	70
Latin America				*52.5*	54.2	55.9	57.7
Southern and South-East Asia			52.9	*65.2*	69.9		69.7
Western Asia						43.2	
Transition countries						20.7	22.6

Notes: Figures in italics are based on too few countries to be representative; data does not always come from the same countries over time; data gathering and methodology for estimation varies over time.

Source: Charmes (2016, table 1.1, p 22)

it was in the 1990s. This is big picture stuff. Clearly these are big categories, enormous regions with great variation within them, and over time. It looks like informal employment is increasing across the board. But taking a more detailed look at one region, North Africa (Table 6.2), it's clear that there is variation between places. It is also clear that there is not a single track (from more to less informal employment), but great variation between nations. Charmes[12] uses this data to show that the informal economy is counter-cyclical, that is, it rises when economic growth declines. For example, Tunisia's structural adjustment programmes, begun in the mid–1980s, mean that by the mid-1990s, the informal economy is larger. Northern Africa is notable as the region with by far the smallest proportion of women in the informal economy (16.4 per cent in the 2005-10 period), half that of the next smallest proportion (33.2 per cent in post-socialist transition countries). That is tiny compared to the 51.1 per cent in sub–Saharan Africa.

In developed countries, different kinds of data are modelled (Tables 6.1 and 6.2 show employment, but Table 6.3 shows estimated per cent of GDP). For comparison, I note that the informal sector contributes 36.6 per cent of GDP in sub–Saharan Africa; 35.8 per cent in Northern Africa; 54.2 per cent in India; 29.2 per cent in Latin America; and 19.5 per cent in transitional economies.[13] So Table 6.3 shows that the informal sector in developed countries is considerably smaller, with the obvious caveat about measurability.

Table 6.2: Employment in the informal economy as a percentage of total non-agricultural employment by five-year periods in Northern Africa

	1975-79	1980-84	1985-89	1990-94	1995-99	2000-04	2005-10	2010-14
Northern Africa	39.6		34.1		47.5	47.3	53.0	50.2
Algeria	21.8		25.63		42.7	41.3	45.6	40.7
Morocco		56.9				67.1	78.5	70.1
Tunisia	38.4	35.0	39.3		47.1	35.0	36.8	40.2
Egypt	58.7		37.3		55.2	45.9	51.2	49.6

Source: Charmes (2016, table 1.2, p 24)

Table 6.3: Informal economic activity as a percentage of GDP, selected 'developed' countries

	2003	2009	2016
EU average	22.6	20.1	17.9
Highly developed non-EU average	12.2	10.1	8.3
Bulgaria	35.9	32.5	30.2
Estonia	30.7	29.6	25.4
Spain	22.2	19.5	17.9
Australia	13.7	10.9	9.8
UK	12.2	10.1	9.0
Austria	10.8	8.5	7.8
Japan	11.0	9.5	8.5
US	8.5	10.1	5.6

Notes: Unweighted averages; Countries ordered by size of informal sector in 2016; EU countries selected from list of 28 member states at intervals from top to bottom of distribution; highly developed countries selected to reflect geographical range.

Source: Selected data from Schneider (2016)

This table suggests that informal economic activity is decreasing in importance in more developed countries. Only the US does not show a regular pattern of decline, but greater variability between the years studied. But there are real reasons to be cautious about reading too much into the actual numbers – different techniques can produce quite different numbers, and by its nature, informal economy activity is hard to assess.

Everyday grey economies

Individuals and households mingle formal and informal work. In a lot of research this is deemed 'a strategy', sometimes 'for survival'. 'Strategy' is not my preferred description, with its implications of autonomous rational decision–making, military or business manoeuvrings. I think that the interconnections between kinds of work are less deliberate than that implies: what is possible matters, what infrastructures, discourses and materials are to hand matters. Living in the urban spaces that AbdouMalique Simone has studied[14] means ducking and diving, bouncing with the balls that come at you, making use of what's on offer – what people and spaces make possible.

Neighbourhoods are a retail opportunity. You might collaborate with a neighbour today to avoid the gaze of a city official, but argue with them tomorrow, entertaining your fellow neighbours in the process. A repertoire of wily tricks is a better option than formalisation, rationality, or promoting the incursion of capitalism. You might negotiate with others, and then have to deal with the dependencies that emerge. In Bangkok and in Jakarta, cities are not only made of the concrete, steel and glass skyscrapers of neoliberal capital, and the hypermobile, connected knowledge workers. There is a way of life tangential to that aesthetic and that set of economistic values. This kind of ordinary living can be found all over the world; in the car boot sales, favours for friends and agreements between neighbours complaining about landlords, sorting and recycling household waste.

To put it another way, studying work as an abstraction makes it easy to forget the way life is made possible through all kinds of work and non-work activities, whose commodification and decommodification isn't set in stone. It may be a moment's wonder or a longstanding strategy. It may be legal or not – or it may be both, as for cash-in-hand work that is hidden from the state to get around tax, social security purposes or to avoid labour laws such as those to do with health and safety, national insurance, or the minimum wage, but offers otherwise legal goods and services for payment. It sounds casual and intermittent in Simone's work, but of course it may well be highly organised. Consider the grey or shadow economy that makes possible the trade in drugs. Agricultural workers grow opium in closed communities that are contracted, regulated and controlled; heroin is a global product manufactured and sold through thoroughly organised shadow economies. For example, in north-east Kyrgyzstan, village life is constituted around the transformation of wild hashish into a cash crop to deal with the uncertainties that emerge through reliance on food agriculture.[15]

One common and kind of intuitive claim made about the spread of neoliberalism is that the logic of the market has spread into more domains of social life, and more is commodified than ever before. However, the story is more complicated. Some activities have been decommodified, that is, they are no longer done for payment, others have been consumer-fied (the 'work' that consumers do to build furniture bought at Ikea, for example) and some things have not been transformed into commodities. Colin Williams[16] suggests that ready claims of increasing commodification and hence increasing formalisation can't be trusted.

Most unpaid work is self-provisioning, and much of the rest is community work. This has remained at a fairly similar level in the post-war period in developed countries: around 50 per cent of work time is unpaid.[17] Some kinds of work, therefore, seem to resist being commodified. In addition to exchanges that are not monetised (for example, volunteering, unpaid reciprocity), there are exchanges that are not profit motivated but that use different notions of value. Only some paid informal work is low-paid market-like work conducted for the purpose of economic gain. This counters stereotypical assumptions that cash-in-hand work in deprived areas is characterised by low-paid and exploitative forms of organisation and in affluent areas it tends to be composed of more autonomous and better paid forms – self-employment, for example. A large amount is done by friends, relatives and neighbours under non-market relations. It is motivated by redistribution and sociality in 'a hidden economy of favours'.[18] This reflects how households make use of many modes of production, move between using formal and informal economic forms, and goods/services are not straightforwardly 'fixed' in one sector. Once informal work is understood as diverse, then it no longer makes sense to think of it as something to eradicate. It is this kind of space that thinking about informal work and informal economic activity brings forward, a set of simple and mundane examples of how work makes realities in the world.

Migrant lives, migrant vulnerabilities

Work moves to workers through offshoring.[19] Workers move to work through migration. Migrant workers move long and short distances in search of seasonal, temporary or permanent work. Despite much of the media rhetoric, they are far from being free to cross borders to steal 'native' jobs: migration is controlled by states, and this kind of control affects how migrant workers find work and how they are treated at work. In my mind at the moment is the point I made in Chapter Two about telling stories about changes to work as though only the organisation of production matters (for example, the move from Fordism to post-Fordism). Without understanding how work relations and work processes are racialised, ethnicised and gendered, then we cannot really get to grips with contemporary working life. Visa points systems and guest worker programmes see nation-states trying to fill the demand for skilled work without making promises about citizenship, with implications for the 'brain drain' in sender places. Migrating for work, with credentialised skills in an in-demand field is one kind of experience, quite different from the 'production first' view of global capitalism which stresses offshoring or migration of production workers. The 'reserve army of labour' keeping wages low (Marx bears responsibility for the original military metaphor) has been used in contemporary writing in fairly thoughtless ways that do not consider the many ways in which migration does and does not happen, the widely different migration pathways, and the histories and geographies that affect those. They are often too readily glossed as an indicator of a rather undifferentiated migrant group. Seeing people only as workers, it can't hint at how people and places are changed by migration (culture and aesthetics matter as well as work), and so reorganising work through migration changes realities.

The work and life of a migrant worker is affected by their migration status (including the kind of work permit), labour relations (including how they are treated in relation to non-migrant workers) and sector-specific features (for example, the seasonality of agricultural work, the unacknowledged social skills needed by service workers). Having marginalised social identities – vulnerable to the insults of those who agree with that increasingly common, angry and aggressive politics that brews up fear of the other – is in part an outcome of state policies towards migrant workers. Indeed, policies that ban or try to limit migration tend to make the lives of actual migrants worse. Immigration controls in the UK shape the categories of migrant so that high- and low-skilled migrants are treated differently.[20] Immigration controls affect employment relations and as a result, make uncertainty normal. Those controls – said to be about protecting new entrants from trafficking and protecting local workers from 'unfair' competition – contribute to the precarious lives of migrant workers. For example, the kind of work permit someone is given affects whether they can move jobs, and so whether they dare complain about bad treatment. New migrants, less certain, less networked, and perhaps less comfortable with speaking a second language, may be 'more reliable' workers because they are less likely to complain. They may pay a cut of their wages to recruitment agents, and they may not be able to do anything about betrayals of their (limited) rights. Of course, migrant workers do not only do informal work, but when they do the effects are shocking. Most migrant workers in Europe end up in sectors that aren't readily outsourced to the Global South but that are deregulated and rely on cheap labour.[21] Construction, agriculture and services make use of informal contracts. This work is '3D: Dirty, Dangerous and Demanding', says Mojca Pajnik, who calls these workers the 'wasted precariat', a phrase that evokes Santos' sense of those who are not deemed to count.[22]

How a Brazilian family manages when their father's main income is from him migrating to do seasonal work in a biofuel plantation gives some insight into the effects of informal work on being able to live.[23] Only the father is employed because of gendered norms around hard manual work and caring responsibilities; his wife and children could travel with him, or may stay behind. If they move together, the mother might find a bit of informal work, often cleaning and washing; the children might go to school. Incomes are uncertain from day to day and across the year, and it's a risk to pay for the whole family to move. Conditions of work are often incredibly hard and dangerous. Were the family to move into the formal economy, though, their conditions might not be much better. Moving into cash-cropping coffee production, for example, can provide a more stable income than subsistence farming, but makes them vulnerable to fluctuations in coffee prices, and to powerful intermediaries and global coffee brands – problems which fair-trade and similar strategies don't entirely alleviate. If you grow cash crops, you have to buy food, which is both a new kind of work and another kind of vulnerability to the market. As it is, the long hours in season, the absence of work out of season, the gendered reasoning that actively makes the household labour essential to subsistence made invisible, show how entwined are issues of work organisation, interconnection between modes and the making of everyday lives.

Both home and work

What image does working at home conjure up? It seems liberating, freeing those who do it from commuting, or from office politics. Wi-Fi technology makes it possible for a networked worker to Skype in pyjamas from their kitchen desk or email from the airport lounge. They are the footloose workers of a friction-free capitalism, doing the high-discretion, autonomous, high-skilled work beloved of knowledge economy policies. Perhaps they have responded to the loneliness of homeworking by joining a co-working space; perhaps they are 'mumpreneurs' pursuing their 'passion'. Technology's downside: producing a worker who is always switched on[24] might get in the way, but the promise of autonomy that is seen as constituting good work can't be denied. Even so, some of these tech-enabled and apparently autonomous workers are likely to be doing crowdsource work that varies from intensely monotonous activities that computers can't do, accessed via Amazon's Mechanical Turk or similar platforms, to rather more engaged and skilled design work where the economy of reputation and the labour arbitrage that is designed into the platforms might nonetheless combine to make for a tough working life. So it certainly isn't a case of pyjama-collar good, blue-collar bad.

The other side of the story about home work is the hidden workforce of manufacturers, mostly but not only women, often part of the majority world. They are doing work that offers them little discretion in how the task can be carried out. Sewing, taking in laundry, cooking and other micro-market domestic tasks are recognisable ways in which women have earned money in many times and places, and point to the importance of recognising norms of domestic labour and household finances at different stages of the lifecourse, as well as the meanings of home, marriage, parenting, (in)equality. Piecework manufacture in the home is also important.

In the 1980s, Maria Mies and colleagues described a process of 'Housewifisation' to make sense of the interconnections of what they described as a global, gendered division of labour.[25] The argument was that transnational corporations actively challenged the power of trade unions and a male-dominated labour force accustomed to collective bargaining, to push for flexible employment. This would involve making more of the hidden, shadow economy comprised of the 'housewife' work of women (as 'workers, breeders and consumers' everywhere), plus the work of less developed former colonies, plus the work in informal sectors (and the value extracted from nature). Housewifisation devalues women's work, sees women as cheap and docile labour for factories in SEZs, or home-based piece workers. The housewife ideology that assumed that women focused mostly on home and were only interested in a bit of extra cash from paid work obscured how central cheap female labour became to global production. Housewifisation is seen when women make making electronics components at home and sell them to intermediary production companies. They are the informal workers most invisible in the supply chains for branded, corporate goods and services. As well as this production work, there are other small-scale informal sectors that matter: agriculture, tourism, services and the sex industry.

Homeworkers are more likely to be women, and do home-work in combination with domestic tasks. Those who work regularly for employers are more visible than own-account workers, or those who do occasional orders. They might often move between sectors, according to what work is available — from sewing to putting together electronics (these need different skills, but the idea that piece work production is unskilled is more to do with the social construction of poor women as unskilled than it is a reflection of the work), and they may also work outside the home, perhaps in service work or agriculture. While home-work covers a range of activities, and what counts as a 'home' varies between cultures, affecting the meaning and feelings of working at home, home-work is nonetheless easy to hide, easy to delete, easy to take for granted. It is part of the urge for flexibility (including by people working out how to live) and it challenges assumptions about linear time and discrete spaces for work. Given all this contingency, it gets much harder to develop a simple answer to what's wrong with work. In order to bring out the ethical issues of informal home-work, we have to understand what is this work like, what does it rely on and what relies on it?

Sewing

Garment production might be assumed to be more of a feature of SEZs in East Asia, specifically the greater Mekong, or the Export Zones of Mexico – both of which are well known for their contribution to the global production of consumer goods. In accounts of global production and global work, Africa is less considered than other areas, and differences between countries in the continent have not been not adequately recognised. Garment production in South Africa, however, sees past colonialism and apartheid as part of the present ongoing racialisation of work. Migration from neighbouring countries is another important influence on how formal–informal activity is organised. The story here is not about a new precariat, formed through enforced flexibilisation – that's a story that applies to the Global North. Theorising from the US has its limits, as discussed in Chapter Five. It's more a question of the effects of a developmentalist state, racialised class dominance, and a large and differentiated group of urban poor (formal workers, informal workers and unemployed), with new migrants entering. The labour market in South Africa as comprised of three zones: formal employment, marked by a racial division of labour and by hierarchy; a non-core sector with minimal protections, that includes outsourced, unskilled work, often part-time work, and domestic service – which is common; and a peripheral zone of informally organised subsistence work, unemployment, work for survival.[26] The social characteristics of workers affect their work situations; gender, race, ethnicity, migration and age matter more than class.

Garment production in Johannesburg is dominated by undocumented migrants, more often male than female.[27] The comparatively stable, regulated jobs in 'full package manufacturers' have decreased in number. These are small firms taking regular orders from retail chains for end products; these firms are more likely to be unionised and more likely to have South African citizens employed (those who make the end product). Other firms doing 'CMT' (cut, make, trim) are subcontracted, irregularly. With even lower quality of life, tiny firms – often groups of men with similar migration trajectories – work together. Undocumented workers cannot register businesses and so can't easily grow. They remain stuck in survivalist mode, doing work for local sales rather than international brands. Around garment production is a range of other informal economy activity: care work, food sales, hairdressing, animal husbandry and recycling. People are making a living out of work when they can get it, and using religious organisations to keep connections with home and make them in the new place.

That old thread: domestic service and care

Men and women do different kinds of informal activities with different contractual arrangements, and the rate at which they do them differs between places (affected, for example, by cultural ideas about whether women should work outside the home). Behind such an obvious point, however, lies a whole range of diversity. How could it be otherwise: how people live affects and is affected by how and where they work. Men's informal activity is significant, especially in informal employment. Women's informal work is less likely to involve employment. Understanding both shows interdependencies within families and the movements between different kinds of formal and informal economic activity.

In Chapter Three, I talked about domestic service as hidden work and asked whether starting from work as care generates a more inclusive understanding. I'll return now to thinking more about domestic service and its relationship to themes in this chapter about interconnections of work, and about class, gender and migration in the making of everyday life. The migration experience of domestic service workers varies. Some cross a border each day or week, like the Hungarian women who make beds and clean toilets in Vienna; others move within a country from a rural to urban setting.[28] State-supported cross-border migration for long periods gets more attention. Indonesia, the Philippines and Sri Lanka trains women to travel overseas to provide domestic service in Hong Kong, Singapore, Malaysia, Taiwan and Australia, among other places. Women from Bangladesh and Pakistan work for employers from Arab countries, moving with them when they travel (to the US, to the UK).

What is going on here? Women do domestic labour, and so women do domestic service work. In the intimate, tense settings where they work, 'migrant domestic workers, whether different in terms of citizenship, ethnicity or rural upbringing, now constitute a social "other", subordinate directly to their employers and more generally to the urban host society'.[29] Threats, violence, control and exploitation are part and parcel of this othering. Domestic service workers might leave their own children in the care of grandparents or other family members, in order to care for stranger-children, remitting money for education and living expenses. This is commonly explained using the idea of a 'care deficit' in the Global North, where women do paid work and don't have time to do domestic work – and any male partners are absolved from responsibility. That kind of explanation assumes a heterosexual family form, and no societal or state interest in caring differently, say, by increasing the status of care and paying more for it. Indeed, nation-states in both sending and receiving countries facilitate migrant domestic work. Special visa categories may ease migration, however, but make the migrant woman vulnerable, for example, by making residency conditional on staying with an employer, controlling access to citizenship status. Once again, the gendering and racialisation of work and migration status contribute to the absence of citizenship rights. Migrant workers are pulled by the promise of paid work, and pushed by the absence of work at home.

In sender countries, it's not unusual to hear public resentment of the women who have abandoned their own families,[30] no matter that remittances are a significant part of GDP, contribute to lower unemployment and are a response to changes to economic structures. Children's resentment of their mother's departure is an understandable and tragic element of this; men's resentment at not being the primary wage earner seems less sad. Nonetheless, for migrant workers, for their families, the emotional pressures of the work are clear. What does it feel like to cuddle someone else's child when your own children are 1,000 miles away? Being a transnational family isn't easy.

In domestic spaces, inequalities of class, gender, culture, race and citizenship affect how domestic servants and employers negotiate over work tasks, feelings and power. Cleaners, nannies and maids create status for their employers by freeing them from doing drudgework, and from a degrading proximity to dirt. Here is one clear example of the importance of thinking about work not solely in contractual terms but in relation to its social presence and effects. Domestic service campaigns sometimes argue that protecting domestic service workers and reinforcing employment rights and employment status can best assure security, that is, by taking forward the idea that home-based work is work. However, a good experience for a domestic worker is less affected by their employment contract, and more by the employer's behaviours and attitudes.[31] An employer who grants the domestic worker some freedom to determine their work themselves and who doesn't impose emotional relationships with family members is most desired. It's hard to regulate in such intimate settings, where the work is out of sight, where the worker is legally, socially and economically powerless.

Personal services

Childcare, healthcare, food provisioning and other kinds of service work are institutionalised differently in different times and places. Other informal services are commonly done outside the home, including sex work. Like domestic service, these kinds of services trouble the cultural boundaries around what it is normal and acceptable to pay for and what should be given as a gift.[32] The ethical issue of what commodification does to social relationships is surrounded by piles of worthless rock, in Fassin's terms, of the different forms that informal activity can take, and the different assumptions about, say, emotional labour, intimacy, trust and care that are entangled there, as well as about what kind of recompense an informal worker gets. As Sarah Sharma[33] says, having sat with taxi drivers wishing and hoping to get busy with fares, these personal services are precarious and informal, extracting long hours for unpredictable reward from the workers to ease the lives of the wealthy executives too busy to wait. Even the unpaid exchanges of personal services, seemingly free of the taint of marketisation, and whether informally organised as favours between mates or mediated and monitored (as in timebanking) bring with them ethical issues around what is being offered, and how.

Have you ever been to a sales party, where a friend has set themselves up as an agent for a company's products? Here, informal sales work mobilising family and friendship ties. Global corporations like Avon — with all the standard accoutrements of a global corporation — brand proposition, supply chain and shareholders — are deliberately informalised on the ground. Their sales representatives rely on getting commission. The Brazilian firm, Natura, which stresses its green credentials, is an example of the blurred boundaries between work and consumerism. The sales reps get the chance to buy products cheaply to try them out.[34] Some do the work so that they can consume the toiletries. But they have to pay upfront without guarantees that they will sell their stock. Their chance of selling out relies on the free work they do to promote the brand, and on co-opting those around them as buyers. In this informal work, social relations become market relations.

These examples help, I think, in putting the gig economy into a broader context. By bringing forward domestic services and putting them next to other kinds of personal services outside the home and relating them to how different kinds of work are connected, a new perspective on the gig economy starts to emerge. A readymade meal, or a quick bite at a local café, or a takeaway ordered through an app and delivered by bike, are all caught up in all kinds of connections with other social and economic processes. There is a more or less intricate supply chain, work happens at different points, the formal and informal meet and part. Innovations in the organisation of work – like platform apps for personal services – can seem to acquire superpowers and transform life (and what they could do can get confused with what they should and will do). My reading tells me that informal work extends beyond the IT-enabled changes to produce a gig economy. Understanding the implications of informalisation means asking about how longstanding service work done by (often poor) women all across the world can be taken for granted and doesn't start looking like a problem when young, white men in post-industrial nations do it.

Respecting complexity

The struggle to measure informal work, which comes about because of its diversity, the way it is hidden from view and the way it raises questions of what work even means, brings to the forefront the great contingency of knowledge about work and hence claims about the ethics of work. How, if it's not immediately clear what work is, can we even think about what it should be like? It's a reminder that definitions and abstractions create easy solutions that, by excluding complexity, exclude experience. Measuring something as mattering, as growing or decreasing is a way to make something into a problem, and so has a pragmatic use, but this is also its limitation.

Informal activities are characterised by precarious and unstable working conditions, limited or absent regulation, and little or no protection for workers. That might make it seem that informal sector jobs are worse than formal sector jobs, although low-quality jobs are common in the formal sector too. It was once common sense that economic development is the way to remove informal work and hence improve working conditions (even though formal work may not be less miserable). Chile and Brazil have recently instituted policies to move away from the informalisation that results from losing the race to the bottom (which is not the same informalisation that grants a bit of flexibility and a bit of autonomy to make a life). Other experiments suggest that regulatory solutions have to bubble up. Formal established unions were able to offer little to homeworkers in Bulgaria and Turkey. Instead, smaller associations have emerged. These start by understanding how homeworkers understood their work activities, and then work out suitable interventions.[35] As regulatory changes intended to develop marketisation and commodification intensify uneven development, then countervailing responses emerge – or are already present in affecting the reception of such regulatory initiatives. To put it another way, informal activity is affected by what the formal economy offers and how it is organised, and by how life exceeds and is not reducible to economic practices. The hidden economy of favours points to the limits of arguments that the world is ever more commodified and that everything is marketised. Non-exchange work is still present – indeed, it might be engendered by the formalisation policies – and it contributes to building and maintaining infrastructure, to providing many kinds of care and to making other kinds of work possible.

SEVEN

Technology

Introduction

Technorationality, a cousin of the monolithic conceptualisation of 'The Economy' as a special space, is a common theme in talk about work at the moment, especially in those horror stories called 'The Robots Are Coming'. This vision of social and economic change driven by the inexorable march of technological progress has a certain appeal, based on ideas that progress generated by science, rationality and logic is morally and practically good. It also has a seductive charge for commentators on work, thrilled to be scared of a future where human workers are not needed. Luddite objections could be made: that this march of progress is not at all desirable. I am drawn to make a pragmatist's objection: that this techno–dominance is a promise of a smooth, error-free future that is based on a pretence that software works, that IT delivers its promises, that putting a machine in the place of a human worker can be done smoothly without generating other kinds of work. It won't break down or need routine repair work (software updates), and it will substitute for labour effectively. It's not that I think new (computer) technologies have not and will not change work. But the idea I borrowed from Santos to think about an expansive present, rather than about an abstract future, and my understanding of the complicated effects of computerisation so far, makes me suspect that the promised future of automation (for example) denies the present complexity. It denies the expertise that make computers useable. The promises of tech are aimed at the present and are performative combinations of fear and seduction, creating beliefs in technocratic power and fear for jobs. It is also a seduction into a dysfunctional relationship, one where the 'user' is constantly updating and working on updated software, constantly having to make corrections in their own behaviour to suit the machine, and yet always believing that the machine is the one in the right, that they are lucky to be part of a relationship that brings them the glorious future right now. IT consultants who persuade managerial staff to re-engineer work processes around new, perhaps unproven, software or hardware, are agents of seduction. It's clearly seen in managerial-bullshit ideas such as the pursuit of 'disruptive innovation', change for change's sake.

This chapter starts by thinking about technologies as part and parcel of a world shaped by human societies, looking at how IT work is gendered and racialised. It then considers the ways in which IT shapes work, and focuses in particular on what computer software work does in the world. Recent discussion of technology and work has focused on automation. I'll discuss the automation of work, and of the forms of control of work that try to slot human work into production processes, with feelings and toilet breaks monitored to make sure that they stay positive and on track. But I consider automation debates to be limited by their mis-readings of what software can do. I explore healthcare as a way to think about the complexity of IT's effects in work. Healthcare is hyper-technologised not least through biotechnology, and is also highly reliant on skilled and caring people, and on administrative and accounting technologies. It reveals the limitations of software.

Technology, work and bodies

In the book so far, I've talked a lot about different technologies, including sewing machines and washing machines, photocopiers and robots. There are a whole array of mundane technologies and ordinary tools – tape guns for sealing cardboard boxes, pallets for stacking that make it possible to transport new products; the combs, scissors and lotions that the hairdresser needs; and the telephones and headsets of call centre BPO staff – that are technologies that are essential for doing different kinds of work. Tools, machines and technologies get normalised and disappear into the background, even becoming infrastructure (as discussed in Chapter Four). In this chapter, I look mostly at computer technologies (a pretty enormous field), and specifically at software. IT is heterogeneous, and 'software' covers an enormous array of phenomena.

I don't accept the assumptions often made in discussion about the effects of technology on work, especially about the effect of IT, that IT is a unified, coherent and consistent thing and has a consistent effect on other practices (and is not itself affected by those other practices). I find the fetish of the present and future to be especially disturbing in historically and technologically naïve discussions of algorithms and platforms. These software products appear in discussions as objects with no history. The products are visible, but the hidden and deleted software work that constitutes them is invisible. The data structures on which they depend, as well as the broader assemblage of practice and objects on which they rely, get ignored. For example, smartphones, key to the 'always on' knowledge worker, are nothing special without a complex array of interdependent pieces of software, as well as a phone and Wi-Fi signals. That, in turn, means an infrastructure of phone masts, electricity and an array of organisations and markets.

The concepts that can be used to think about these questions once again affect the kinds of stories that are told. In this chapter, more explicitly than in other chapters, non-human entities are key, understood using the idea of the 'social shaping of technology'.[1] Thinking about technology using these kinds of ideas avoids making the mistake of seeing technology as determining social life, condemning it to follow technology's inescapable internal logic, and it avoids only thinking about technology as *having an impact on* rather than being shaped by social (and economic, cultural and political) milieu. By refusing a position that technology entirely produces social life, and an equally weak position that technology is only ever the product of social and political choices, it is possible to see how technological changes are negotiated, not always consciously, and how decisions that stabilise particular outcomes close down other possibilities. This ends the twin fictions that technology is either merely a neutral tool in the hands of agentic humans, or that humans must follow the compelling technical imperative. In thinking about social–material entanglements as they emerge in specific contexts through the movements of different kinds of actors, technological workers and the grey technologies that affect work, as well as the headline news about automation, come into view. Further, the expansionist tendencies of computing technologies raise questions about the ethics of powerful IT, for example.

Technology shapes (work) inequalities

Cynthia Cockburn's comment that 'women may push the buttons but they may not meddle with the works'[2] set the scene for discussing the gendering of technology at work. She was describing how new computer technologies in the printing industry led to the replacement of male craft workers with semi-skilled female operatives and a single male system technologist. The early years of computing tell a similar story about gendering and hierarchy in technology work.[3] ENIAC, one of the first computers, was built by the American military, initially as a device for calculating shell trajectories. It later became a component of the Manhattan Project (and this is not the only connection between technologies of work, technologies of war and technologies of leisure). Pictures of ENIAC, EDSAC and other early machines are now used as the butt of 'look how far we've come' jokes about linear progress towards the glorious present where computers fit in pockets instead of taking up entire rooms.

At first, producing hardware seemed more challenging than machine operation. (Male) electrical engineers made hardware and 100 young, mathematically able women were assigned the clerical work of programming, on the assumption that programming was just a kind of typing. Programming ENIAC turned out to be tricky: the women had to learn the logics of the machine and its circuitry, by crawling around the machine. As it became clearer that sorting the hardware was a fairly ordinary engineering problem, and software was where the real challenge lay, because the potential for error was greater, more and more men did programming work. Changes to computer programming from the 1950s can be interpreted as a familiar story about how craft work gets packaged up into different roles, with fewer, well-paid men doing the complicated, intellectually demanding and creative overview work such as systems programming and analysis, and larger numbers of less well-paid people doing distinct tasks using 'canned programmes' (off-the-shelf solutions to common data processing requirements). Some functions were added as part of the hardware of machines, others were (software) programs that could be used consistently between machines. The work processes were stabilised in different ways, and this is central to the dramatic transformation of many kinds of work. Personal computers, spreadsheets, logistics tools and so on emerge from this. Computer technicians, like the electrical engineers they once were, 'were skilled workers whose job was to use science to render the skills of other workers unnecessary'.[4] Brain work was separated from the grunt work of the coder in a process similar to how making other objects was fragmented by assembly line technologies. However, this Bravermanian deskilling story somewhat underplays the emergence of new kinds of work and new combinations of skilled work.

The hierarchies between analyst, programmer and coder has always been imperfect and fairly arbitrary (not least because of the fluidity and creativity of job titles). Indeed, the question of what programmers did, and what programmers could do for business, were extensively discussed in US corporations in the 1960s, as programming started to reconfigure work processes and management hierarchies.[5] Now ideas from computing (for example, about networks and workgroups) are used to explain the organisation of computing work and many other kinds of work. The Silicon Agenda of 'agile computing' has spread into 'agile management', for example. Contemporary IT occupations are further differentiated, including through the ways that technical and interpersonal skills are combined in some kinds of roles, including consultancy, client servicing, project management and so on, not least because of the negotiation necessary in outsourcing. Technological work is 'culturalised' as these 'soft' (feminised) skills emerge.

The story of the gendering of computer programming and its relationship to male-dominated electrical engineering and female-dominated administration shows how technologies reflect and reproduce gendered scripts. Changes to work are related, but not reducible, to technological change; technology here is shaped in relation to gender. Gendered attributes of technology come to be incorporated in the stabilisation of other technologies, as when specific scripts such as 'easy to use' are attributed as features of domestic technologies that are aimed at women.[6] That's not to say that social interests are straightforwardly injected into machines, but that thinking about who the user is and what they are like is part of the process of design, and that affects how technologies emerge. What the user can do is therefore already imagined and already constrained. Comparable processes are seen when work technologies are designed to be 'idiot proof' by IT engineers who know best. I'll return to this question about 'idiot-users' in the discussion of healthcare technologies.

Body shopping

I have talked previously about gender as intersectional with race. Considering IT in relation to older technologies shows that the racialisation of work processes in IT also has echoes in longer entrenched inequalities that technology has supported. As Daniel Rood has recently argued, racial divisions of labour in the Americas in the 1840s and after 'were reengineered in response to the incorporation of new machinery. Conversely, new technologies were shaped by notions of racially endowed aptitudes for different kinds of work'.[7] This period of slavery, where plantation complexes were globally connected via commodity exchange, was made possible through two kinds of interconnected expertise: that which contributed to the development of new technologies (which was sometimes expertise held by slaves and non-European managers), and that which was based on claims to be able to manage machines and slave labour in order to extract maximum value. This is one of several possible examples that reveal technology as an active participant in building unequal treatment of people.

I could pick any number of other moments to show that technology is racialised. For example, the recruitment of young women into factory work was a crucial part of the 'manufacturing miracle' of Asian middle-income countries in the 1980s. These electrical production and assembly workers were cheap, and considered mild and nimble fingered; stereotypes of deferential and pliable Asian women mattered, however untrue. This new work changed where and how people lived. It created new kinds of informal economic activity.[8] Illicit, fake-branded electronics goods were assembled in small shops near-ish to formal economy production units in Kolkata, making use of the knowledge of skilled workers. They were made with imported components assembled by temporarily employed unskilled female labour, and sold by men who also offered repair services. Here is the informal sector connected to outsourcing in an unevenly globalised world. Hardware isn't the only story to tell. IT-enabled service provision, as in the offshore call centre, tells us a lot about the modes of interconnection between work.[9]

Technologies and infrastructures make it seem like distance doesn't matter, but apparent globalisation is possible only because of the continuation or re-creation of differences between places. The difference of labour costs, of state regulation, of labour control and so on, mark and influence the move. So, too, does political history (for example, the history of colonisation and the marks it leaves on culture) that facilitates the move, for example, through the chances of finding English speakers. In current times, the fear in the west of the threat to 'good' service jobs from middle-income countries with educated, technically skilled workforces who are going to 'steal' knowledge economy jobs, is a macro-level manifestation of racialisation. Moral panics of 10 years ago about offshore call centres are now joined by fear of the Indian coder.

This speaks again to the issues of uneven development raised in earlier chapters. Aneesh[10] uses the evocative phrase 'body shopping' to refer to the practices of US software companies buying in software engineers from India. This is basically agency work, made possible by further and higher education institutes in India producing future workers with technical skills. More recently, however, instead of moving the bodies, software companies have been moving the work. From technical support, to software development, to design and animation, and many kinds of business processing services, communications software makes it possible for US clients to be serviced by Indian workers. The work migrates, but the worker doesn't, on the assumption that the technology and social relations can be seamlessly translated. Microsoft India, based in Bangalore, for example, can recruit 'two heads for the price of one', in the words of Brian Valentine, a Microsoft Senior Vice President.[11] 'Routine' computing work gets 'offloaded' to software workers in the Philippines, following precise instructions laid down by American staff.[12] Managers in the Philippines still had to debug the American work, but these 'grinder' projects were done more cheaply outside the US. Indeed, a range of routine tasks that could have been given to machines were given to the offshored workers. The tacit skills of human judgement were desirable so long as they were cheap.

Working with IT

I'm interested in IT, but available data covers the broader category of ICT (information and communications technology). Of global employment in the ICT sector, 80 per cent is in China, India, the EU and the US.[13] ICT employment is 8.9 per cent of the total employment in Taiwan, 4.2 per cent in Korea and 3.6 per cent in Japan. These countries also have the most ICT manufacturing.[14] Once again, it's important to be cautious about the kind of data that exists. Different definitions and different measurements abound: this data refers to employment in ICT (information and communications technology) sectors, a broader category than IT, itself broader than software, defined the production of goods and services where 'the function of information processing and communication by electronic means, including transmission and display'.[15]

Data on employment by industrial sectors give only an overview of the significance of computer technologies to work. Data that considers how computer technologies are involved in work provides a deeper insight into the questions of the organisation of work, its interconnections and its effects. Again,

OECD data and EU data are the most respectable sources. More employed workers use the internet at work (notice the shift from measuring ICT to the generic measure 'using the internet'). Over 60 per cent of workers do so in Norway, Korea and the US, for example.[16] More precisely, between 22.8 per cent (in Italy) and 51.5 per cent (Norway) of individuals use communications and information systems (CIS) technologies in their daily paid work every day; from 17 per cent (in Italy and Poland) to 36.6 per cent (in the Netherlands) use office productivity software (OPS).[17] Specialist ICT workers (defined as those where respondents used programming languages every day) are found in obvious occupations – ICT user support, software development and analysis, ICT managers. These amount to around 3.2 per cent of total employment in the EU28 countries.[18] Specialist ICT work is also found in some less obvious occupations. Higher education teachers, engineers, blacksmiths and tool makers, architects and planners, and managers in business services, in manufacturing and in sales and marketing all score highly on the OECD rankings of ICT intensive occupations.[19] These small numbers of specialist workers have significant power over the larger group who use internet, CIS or OPS technologies, as well as over those not measured by these surveys who use IT.

The affordances of software technologies enable new ways of measuring worker effort. The combination of rationalistic models of behavioural science, 'agile management' philosophies and tech companies delight in finding new tricks for IT to perform, regardless of their desirability, has led to patents for wearable technologies that monitor where a warehouse picker's hands are, to add to a range of other surveillance strategies. Biometric measures that include how far back in your chair you sit, the tone of your voice and how you contribute to conversations have been developed by the ironically named Humanyze, an MIT spin out. Some companies, says Phoebe Moore,[20] present this as wellness, and offer consumer wearables to their staff (step counters and the like) to gamify workplace relationships. For Moore the issue is the extension of control and the extraction of value from workers' every living gesture.

The nu-taxi firm Uber not only has tech that keeps a close eye on its drivers; it also gamifies their work to nudge them to work longer. Its response to driver unrest is not to address the ambiguities in the work relationship and labour contract, but to build software tools to change a driver's behaviour. Drivers use an Uber app, which shows them an arbitrary earnings target, gives them the next fare before they've dropped off the current one, and sends messages using a female persona to suggest where the next surge in passengers might come from.[21] This control is perhaps a new version of older scientific management techniques to monitor and measure work. More importantly, though, it shows that measurements of productivity and effort are extensive, bureaucratised, personalised and very ordinary. Further, there are more mundane problems that come from working with IT. Repetitive strain injuries, eyestrain, aching backs and similar show how using IT changes human bodies. Far more research has looked at how work is changed by these technologies; quite a lot less into the work that goes into designing and implementing such technologies.

Giant mechanical brains

In 1949, Edmund Callis Berkeley wrote a book *Giant brains: Or, Machines that think*,[22] perhaps the first of many prophesies to foretell the imminent arrival of computing technology that can master human skills and replace human workers. Of all the ways that technology is affecting work at the moment, the greatest concern in media and policy discussions is the effect that automation will have on jobs, often hyped up as 'robotisation'. The way a debate is framed affects the kinds of ethical questions that need to be asked. Robotisation is just now being made into a problem. It hasn't always been a problem, although processes of robotisation have been in place in factories for some time. Why now? What's being achieved by making this a concern? And what gets made invisible by all the attention to automation? Not only is informal work and care work invisible, but also programming work is deleted. It often seems as if the coming changes are inevitable. For some they are desirable, for others they are frightening, but at the same time rather seductive, creating the kinds of affects that people get from watching horror films in comfortable and air-conditioned cinemas. For yet others, automation brings the promise of liberation from work (at least from the kinds of jobs that are amenable to it, not from the invisible work that makes life possible). Such discussions can tend to downplay the ways automation is already present: it's in the standard formatting of this document and the constraints my word-processing package has placed on me. It's in every spreadsheet, online form, payroll system, EPOS till, CAD programme or sat nav. And more subtley, it is in the rules and regulations followed by many workers: teachers taught to set aims and objectives for each class; researchers with publication and income targets; call centre staff following scripts. As soon as norms are formalised they move from a space of vernacular opportunity, contingent decision-making, exploration and creativity, to a space of borders, limits and automated responses. Still, much of the talk about automation positions it as happening in the future.

The biggest concern with automation is that jobs will be more polarised (paid work is pretty much taken for granted as the work that is worth studying). A small number of high-skilled jobs will stay, including those that are either involved in designing and creating technologies, or that rely on expertise and capacities that are not straightforwardly automatable. A larger number of jobs will disappear or change radically, and the people who might expect to do that work will be unemployed. The lower part of the polarised future might have two layers: jobs that become more routinised as software captures and dictates decision-making (as in the software used in call centres to direct enquiries through pre-determined paths); and jobs that disappear with nothing emerging to provide suitable alternative work for those replaced by robots. It's a grim picture. Polarisation is likely to be geographically differentiated, reflecting and reproducing existing inequalities. The discussion about automation is certainly affected by a level of excited, performative speculation. The 'business case' is that automation in production reduces labour costs, and increases the quality, efficiency and flexibility of production. That is also the 'development' case: automation makes a country competitive. Arguments to support the idea that automation *this time* is brand new include the claim that computer technologies are the dominant form of capital investment, more dominant than any other category of investment ever.[23] Overall, though, there are some good reasons to re-cast this discussion in different terms, to re-imagine what's at stake in order to think differently about the job crisis to come, and about solutions.

We have, after all, been here before:

> ... the new technology is threatening a whole new group of skills — the sorting, filing, checking, calculating, remembering, comparing, okaying skills — that are the special preserve of the office worker... In the end, as machines continue to invade society, duplicating greater and greater numbers of social tasks, it is human labor itself — at least, as we now think of "labor" — that is gradually rendered redundant.[24]

The issue of what the future will be like is at the heart of automation discussions. So much of the discussion is based in a vague futurism about 'the end of work' and the 'rise of the robots'. The vagueness is irritating for a couple of reasons. The first is that it doesn't make space for understanding how what appears to be left for the future is already here in the present (similar to how environmental crisis is talked about as something still to come). The second is that statements about the inevitability of change in the future have vital effects in the present. Words have consequences. In this case, they make the automation feel inevitable, even desirable, producing an infernal alternative. That downplays the other kinds of changes that could also do with some attention, including environmental changes, the persistence of work that does not involve software, and indeed the question of what forms of work (education, healthcare) might not benefit from being transformed by computer technology. That has effects in the present, creating fear for job loss and perhaps, then, acceptance of worse working conditions now. Third, it gets in the way of learning from past changes because it makes the claim that *this time it's different*. If this round of automation is new and distinctive, then analysing trends isn't useful, looking backwards and learning from previous mistakes is pointless. But just as Heilbroner, quoted above, was partly right that some of those calculating and remembering skills would go, other skills on his list have changed, some are resistant to automation, and new ones have emerged. This demands a more nuanced discussion.

In particular, automation debates tend to take a deterministic view of technology and its relationship to labour processes, familiar from the deskilling arguments discussed in Chapter Two, as well as from those who consider technological innovation to be a comfortable bedfellow for neoliberal economic practices. Different conceptual assumptions, though, create different insights, more attentive to the production, maintenance and use of machines, to the material constraints on some actions, and the facilitation of others. The question to ask is not whether robots will take jobs, but how technological change, including IT, continues to change existing work – as it did when Heilbroner was writing, and as it will now. Changing work isn't the same as replacing work, and looking into what happens when new technologies are introduced is instructive for rethinking what technologies do. As I'll discuss in the section on healthcare technologies, new technology causes problems that exceed those it was supposed to solve. And this makes me think that the promised outcomes of future technological changes are not really predictable. Work changes, and paid jobs change, but they do so in relation to other work. There is no 'end of work' because most of what work does to the world is still there. It's important to have discussions which don't assume the inevitability of technology-driven changes, and which consider the kinds of jobs that might disappear, the kinds that might not be amenable to one of the several kinds of automation that could be possible, and what kinds of jobs are needed to work with the machines.

Sorting things out

Work processes, work organisation and the interconnections of work are already affected by the automating practices of software products. Ordinary administrative technologies (for example, as used for audits and financial accounting) are actively involved in making the world they study. They participate in 'sorting things out'.[25] That means, deciding what to count (and so what counts). For example, enterprise resource planning (ERP) software claims to integrate physical production with broad business functions such as sales, finance and human resources. Software developers assemble the firm by converting it into data.[26] Data is analysed into information and translated into knowledge, which returns to transform the 'real world'. But this analysis has unintended effects and demands all kinds of workarounds. The software system has codified and transformed expertise embedded in it. But it then created new expertise among those assigned to interpret that data. The company using it gets reformatted through the technology as basic business processes get adapted to meet the expectations of the software. For those who ended up working in the new streamlined system, the power of the general principle that better data means better decisions was so normal that disagreements were offered with apologies, and scepticism about the new knowledge produced was common. Nonetheless, companies sign off 'multi-million pound IT projects to implement ERP technologies whose benefits themselves are impossible to demonstrate with the kind of calculative precision claimed on behalf of the system by its supporters and developers'.[27]

Believing in software and its power to make a business better is an act of faith that means believing in the 'evil media' – in the grey technologies that are kind of invisible but that shape and format everyday lives in more or less discretely intrusive ways.[28] By valorising technical-rational problem solving, appealing to software workers and managers as rational, good actors who create good, just goals reinforced by professional ethics, it is easy to see how software work gets legitimated and that technical solutions become good solutions.

Work gets configured and reconfigured, and so different kinds of work end up in a different relationship to each other. Algorithms, for example, reconfigure work processes around the specific technical and social conundrums that providing services through software creates[29] across vast digital infrastructures. Filipino workers grind through software problems, and American workers do emotional labour and education work with services users. The figure of the client might loom large, albeit as an abstract figure imagined in the minds of software workers, often as annoying, incompetent or irrational.[30] It is little wonder, then, that software gets made to the worldview of developers taking the position that they are likely to be more right than users. Sometimes this might involve holding clients to ethical standards, say, in relation to what data mining should and shouldn't be used for.[31] On other occasions, as in the story of ERP, reshaping is less positive. Ethical issues and ethical standards are thus sometimes part of how people do work, and the work that makes networks, devices and software that affects the potential ways in which they can be used.

Human plus machine

I recently read a news story about a German bank clerk who counted 1.2 million hoarded coins by hand. It added up to about €8,000.[32] It stuck in my mind because counting machines are well-established substitutes for counting by humans. These coins were old and rusted and wouldn't go through the machines. It's rare now for bank clerks to count coins. Bank workers now do different kinds of work: selling financial products and managing feeling. This example shows that changes to work are not simple replacements of people by machines. The bank worker who counted the coins was able to separate those that were rusted together and identify them because of his motor skills and tacit judgements. Software is very good at work that's based in logical processes. It is great at maths. It is not so good at judgement, and is reliant on what programmers have understood about those processes which they are capturing. It is certainly no good at separating rusty coins. Programmers have to understand the tasks they are trying to get the computer to do, and then they have to programme the computer to do those tasks. Automation relies on translation into a different context (driverless vehicles rely on the road being translated into a map and on sensor technologies that understand environments – adaptation not substitution).

Put like that, it's clear that automation is more challenging than it might at first seem. It is sometimes the case that software programmers *think* they know just what a task is, but they struggle to make the fine-grained judgements. So software programs for diagnosing illnesses can't easily make the distinctions between different illness trajectories that a clinician might make, in part because they rely on standardised classification processes (for example, ICD-10 medical codes), and in part because they rely on tacit knowledge having already been made explicit and then capturable by programmers and so part of the range of options. Part of the effect of 'robots are taking jobs' headlines is to strengthen the hubristic claims of IT to know, understand, translate and reproduce all human endeavours. But looking inside the processes for doing this makes it look less certain. Craft work, common sense, improvisation, judgement, creativity, problem solving, adaptability and feeling aren't done well by computers, and are part of far more jobs and far more kinds of work than the binaristic language of 'skilled and unskilled' work might suggest. It might be reasonable to think that work that can be understood by programmers and translated into computer programs will be easily replaced, even though a replacement is not like-for-like but enrols different processes. And work that is not routine or that relies on tacit knowledge will not readily be co-opted.

Further, software is error-prone and vulnerable. When it fails, it asks people to adapt to it. Through sleight of hand, its errors are made to seem to be caused by users, not by the software itself, and the legacy of design assumptions within it. After all, software companies design work to 'create resilience', for example, errors and problems are introduced deliberately to get people used to dealing with failure, or teams are set in competition with each other. So failures *should* have been dealt with. But they are not always fully imagined in the design process. Error creates the need for data clean up, debugging, reinstallation and technical support. And – ideally – more software.

Doing healthcare

The more that ideas about technology tend towards abstract futurism, the more it matters to think about real instances of technological change in the present. Bringing in work and the making of everyday life through care and repair reminds us of the other things that matter when we understand what work does to the world: robots don't wipe bottoms or give affection. Care labour is implicated in IT technology, and it is intimate work that is often emotionally demanding and often misrecognised as natural 'women's work'; it is a prime example of invisible work. Medical work is the high-status, high-skilled part of care work. It is reliant on a range of technologies, from drugs to heart rate monitors, from electronic patient records (EPRs) to financial accounting software. Healthcare is an intimate problem, an organisational problem, a communication problem, and an accounting problem.

By understanding medical work as arranged around the trajectory of a person's illness, with both physical and organisational elements, it becomes clear that many forms of work are involved in treating an illness and caring for an ill person: technical, clinical, caring and communicative work. Work is organised around accepted (mandated) clinical standards, but also must deal with 'the problematic character of the [illness] trajectories themselves and the host of technological, organizational, and client derived contingencies that beset all those who are doing the trajectory work'.[33] Medical work relies on anticipating potential futures, negotiation with others and responses to events. It relies also on a complicated interplay of technical and social skills and so is one counter to assumptions that technical and social skills relate to different kinds of work. This points again to the limitations of thinking about technical skill solely in relation to managerial control and substitution of workers by machines, as discussed in Chapter Two. That's in part because of how social behaviour and encounters with machines are situated in singular local contexts.

The promises IT makes for a better future often seem to be aimed at disguising the problems of the present. Promises made in the late 1990s about, say, the use of AI in clinical reporting[34] haven't yet come true. More recent promises about how health informatics will benefit record keeping, administration, communication and knowledge acquisition,[35] or current promises that e-health initiatives or wearable technology will solve the problem of the cost of healthcare by replacing treatment with pre-emptive self-care, might or might not come true. Digital health is a magic pill to cure the healthcare crisis: the contemporary equivalent of the magic bullet of antibiotics. The list of possible technologies, at different stages of imagination, design and production, is extensive and it would be easy to be distracted by the ambition on display and seduced by the stories of the technology. Two implications emerge for me. One is that this cynical/careful understanding of IT, including of software, infrastructures, their relationship and the organisational forms around them, makes those promises about automation and robotisation in other work look pretty dubious. The second is that the work of software development, the work of managing in new IT systems, is work that re-makes medical care work. It changes skills and it changes what caring is. New work tasks such as identifying data management and analysis strategies, and cleaning data, emerge; existing administrative and clinical work is changed; technologies reverberate in mundane care settings in private homes, where patients/care recipients learn how to work new machines – or reject the intrusion of new machines in their home, as with patient-at-home technologies trialled in Denmark.[36]

Twenty-six years separate a study of how two comparable radiology scanning machines were institutionalised in different ways in different places[37] and a study of robots being introduced into pharmacies.[38] The technology has changed dramatically, but what the technology does to established ways of working is weirdly similar. Technicians in both settings – radiologists and pharmacists – had to create work-arounds, change their work, make new sense of what the technology could and couldn't do. The robot, for example, could carry some of the pharmacy stock, but pharmacists stocked the same products on the traditional shelves as well, for ease of access. That means two stock monitoring processes and two loading processes. Attempts to automate GP work through natural language processes are limited by GPs disliking autosuggestions and overriding them. In these examples, new technologies change organisational practices, occupational identifications and the encounters that different professionals had with each other. New technology doesn't remove work, it changes it; new systems take time to become invisible parts of everyday care work.

Cures for administrative ills

Old technologies have been transformed by IT. For example, EPRs replaced paper records. Managers and IT engineers talk about the intransigence of clinical staff in the face of new technologies, who may not be part of decision-making processes.[39] But that depends on how different kinds of work are interconnected. In Finland, for example, clinicians are now trained in accounting and finance (which they find easier than medical care) to be able set and run budgets.[40] This generates a hybrid medical and financial organisation where clinicians were involved in costing and pricing. In the British NHS, by contrast, senior clinicians are more likely to leave financial decisions to the finance officer and use clinical legitimacy to justify expenditure as necessary. So while financial and medical costs and outcomes are part of how organisations are assessed – and hence part of the risk management processes of hybrid organisations – the absence of clinical involvement in the financial side causes problems. Different kinds of expertise are assembled differently, and this affects work and care.

Reading about how new healthcare technologies were implemented, I was amazed by how similar research findings are from the 1980s, the 1990s, 2000s and 2010s, to the experience of my study with Andrew Goffey and Ewen Speed.[41] For example, 20 years ago, Brian Bloomfield[42] studied an attempt to set up an IT system to gather population data about patients. He describes the involvement of management consultants in promoting technology as a solution, the fetish of 'information' no matter what can be done with it, management irritation at the intransigence of clinical staff, and the compromises forced on various parties. Time has passed, but the story is the same.

In a context where IT is commonly offered as a solution to problems you didn't know you had, it's no surprise that it is also considered to be the solution to lack of funding and excess of demand for healthcare. We studied work towards an EPR system that could be accessible (and editable) by multiple healthcare providers and by patients, and that could link up to records held by social care and the like. But a legacy of technological underinvestment meant that healthcare workers were reliant on antique computers for some tasks. Interoperability was a struggle in a real-world, creaky IT system where, as is common, old and new technologies were squashed together. But more important was the decision-making process that resulted in the purchase of an off-the-shelf EPR system by clinical managers without involvement of the on-the-ground medical staff or the IT department.

EPR changes how medical staff work on a day-to-day basis, asking them to adapt to what the system demands, that is, to how the software had been made with key work processes translated into database elements. So how software engineers had made translations mattered. Medical staff were configured as users, and their expertise was configured into buttons, dropdown menus and global diagnostic standards. The software is then re-translated by clinical staff, who debug, changing their practice to conform to what the software expects. Preferences for 'good clean data' (that is more amenable to being merged with other 'good clean data' for population level analysis by big data companies) triumphs over clinical nuance. Other companies (although not in the specific case we studied) then gain contracts to make different systems communicate, to reconcile data disparities and omissions, and so on. Doing care work is different when the tool is different, so how the tool is made, the assumptions it contains and what it's made to do really matter. Software has a politics, and its politics affects work.

What problems do technologies solve?

While software promises all kinds of solutions – an 'information revolution', a 'digital economy' – it does not always deliver on these promises. Studies of the effects of technology on jobs outnumber studies that look at how IT is designed and produced by software workers, that consider the assumptions about the world they make and how they translate work activities into programmes. Technologies can substitute work, change how work is organised and change what is involved in doing work. That makes it important to study how technologies, especially software technologies which tend to be black-boxed as unknowable, are made. What goes on when new technology is designed, implemented and left to run wild? I would like a bit less disruptive innovation and a bit more disruption to the assumptions of technological innovation as an unalloyed benefit. Instead, what is needed is a better understanding of what technologies are doing and what effect they have on the problems they seem to be fixing.

EIGHT

Green work

Introduction

The Anthropocene era describes now: a world made by human–economic activity that has fundamentally changed environments. The Anthropocene is a human–induced threat to human life (and to all other life). Dualist philosophy separates nature and culture to make it seem like nature is a resource for human use, and a source of value. That makes humans dominant actors. This is problematic. Decentring humans to understand them as part of natural, technical, informational and economic entities is essential to relearning the position of the human.[1] Decentring unmasks the idea of autonomous human activity and reveals human dependency on nature. Nature affects everyday life in dramatic ways through 'natural' disasters and in routine and habitual ways. It is not a pre-given entity on which humans act. Nature has temporalities and material effects, it incorporates the existence and effects of human and non-human bodies, and it brings the unpredictability of weather, the transforming power of soil, coal and rare earth minerals. Decentring, not dualism, has some important implications. For example, 'natural disasters' such as droughts or floods often have devastating effects because of their economic, political, cultural and technological entanglements with nature, rather than being only natural – or indeed only economic. Perhaps because of the long effects of colonialism that let poverty take hold, or because state infrastructures are not able to cope, some populations are more vulnerable to 'natural' disasters. Calling something a 'natural' disaster makes invisible the social, political and economic entwinings.

Nature emerges in work practices in many ways: as what is worked on and with, as ecological commitments, as the work that makes the world – where wildlife is protected, a toxic plant controlled, a broken supply line is mended, or profit is extracted from a resource. Both how work is organised in relation to nature, and what that work does, is especially important. Often, these questions have been answered using a 'jobs versus environment' framing – whereby either jobs or environment can be protected, but not both – showing that the well-established conflict between labour and capital is transversal with other kinds of conflicts. This shows that when nature and environment are recruited as ethical issues in a discussion of the ethics of work, the conversation gets complicated. One response has been to think about how to protect jobs and the environment simultaneously, which is discussed below in the section on green jobs. That, however, jumps ahead of the important questions about how the environment is affected by how work is organised, by how environments are affected by different kinds of work, and by what work does to nature.

The catastrophic threat to 'business as usual' made by anthropocenic changes has given rise to some intense solutioneering by those who would guard our futures. Ecological modernisation is one such strategy. 'Greening the economy' will involve greening work, and is heralded as a means to address the twin threats of environmental catastrophe and uneven global development. But are green jobs really 'good for the environment and good for the worker'? While green job policies speak strongly of an upskilled workforce doing environmentally beneficial work – for example, builders learning how to retrofit old buildings with energy-saving materials – many green jobs such as recycling work are dirty, dangerous and unskilled.[2] Green work activities exist in the formal and informal economies, they are the targets of public policy, and they are distributed unevenly across the world. They bring the promise of economic development almost as usual, offering a nicer, kinder economy. They rely on the promise of technologisation, in the guise of modernisation, to solve environmental, as well as economic and social, problems.

In this chapter I will explore work in relation to technocratic understandings of ecological crisis. Debates about green jobs are one place where ethical issues about work extend beyond the ethics of the treatment of workers, and so this provides an opportunity for thinking about the broad spectrum of what's wrong with work. However, solutionism is implicit in 'green collar' work, and at work on and with nature and the environment more broadly. It's important to explore possibilities that exceed what technocracy considers credible. Before and after I focus on solutions, I look at ways that working on nature involves and invokes both skill and care, and demands specific ethical orientations to work and to the world.

Working in and with nature

The word 'nature' conjures up images of landscapes, green hills, rocky mountains, white beaches. It sounds rural and romantic. The ethico-aesthetic pull of beauty or of charismatic beasts such as polar bears are powerful feelings that contribute to environmental movements. Romantic though it can be to talk about nature, it's a mistake to think natural entities as solely in need of protection. Invasive weeds that poison bio-diverse landscapes demand eradication work not protection work, for example. Nature and environment are also urban, and environmental damage in cities, such as air pollution produced by industry, or loss of biodiversity generated by building development, is important. In the environmental justice movements, daily life matters, and the care work that is produced by living in a polluted area is an important element of thinking about work in the environment. Human economic actors are enrolled by nature – by weather, by growing seasons – as they participate in economic activity. Working directly with nature and earth brings questions of the ethics of what work does to the world to the fore in a way that is not often thought about. How destructive or sustainable these encounters with 'nature' are is tied up with – but not reducible to – the kinds of economic and technological practices with which they are entangled. We can't understand agricultural work solely by thinking about worker and machine, nor the biological processes that turn seeds to plants. And some occupations see and signal environmental change through the routine work they do. Farmers and wildlife officers do work that is evidently embedded in specific local places. Whereas the assembly line is a space where the search for efficiency through control dominates, the field is a space of excess: unexpected wildlife, seeds that grow alongside weeds, lack of bounty or unexpected bounty, the effects of weather, these all really matter. Agriculture workers can sit up high in a tractor fitted with a GPS to spray pesticides over GM crops planted in fields made big enough for the tractor to turn, or they can plant hedgerows to prevent soil erosion and encourage natural predators, or they can research and test what can be added to overworked and over treated soil: each has different encounters with nature and different effects, but all have to notice change.

Working on and with soil is the (literal) grounding for ecosystems, for the food chain (and all the industrialised and logistical work that stems from that), and for the work of everyday life. Other kinds of nature-work, with obvious ethical implications, make the world as well. Environmental consultants, for example, might be commissioned to check whether airport developments conform to protected species legislation. It is easy to explain this kind of work in capitalocentric framings: these workers are agents of capitalist development, aiming to ease economic development processes by smoothing out diversity. Moore and Robbins[3] raise some questions about that kind of easy reasoning that suggests that capitalism tries to flatten nature, but nature causes trouble. Instead, they look to proliferate diverse accounts and diverse understandings of what ecology does. So the encounters with earth by environmental consultants involve engaging in and with capitalist processes, but that engagement has effects: the airport is built and species are protected. The one doesn't cancel the other, but both exist.

Everyday environments

It's easy to illustrate the importance of care labour in relation to environmental change. Examples abound from sites of industrial pollution: historical incidents like Love Canal or Bhopal still have effects on living bodies; poisoned water in Flint, Michigan and nuclear fall-out in Fukushima have present and future effects. If damage to human and non-human bodies is present, then care work and repair to ameliorate that damage has to emerge too. The fast violence of natural disasters demands that infrastructures get mended. The slow violence[4] that happens where climate change is an everyday lived reality is also damage that demands ordinary care.

Environments entangle care work in other ways too. The care work of food provisioning by shopping in the supermarket for ready meals served in recyclable plastic, or of buying imported avocados to stay healthy, shapes and reshapes local and global environments. Consumption work matters. How nature is treated and how environments change affects what kind of care labour people do; and the organisation of care, as a central part of everyday life or reproduction, affects current and future environmental change. The material practice of care work is affected by mundane technologies that transform everyday life and hence everyday care labour, whether new stoves that mean that women do not have to gather wood[5] or the enormous transformations that go along with an ordinary technology such as refrigeration: new work to pack and transport chilled fresh food, new ideas about cooking and eating.[6] Work, doing things with and to matter, shapes socio-nature.

Earlier discussions about the limits of assuming that paid work counts most also have implications for understanding work in relation to the environment. The work done on nature is gendered, classed and raced. This is certainly the case in forest conservation in Bangladesh.[7] Here, communities who work the land shape the ecosystems they encounter, seeing the daily practices of care for the forest as an affective commitment to the land, landscape, community and self. People patrolled the forest every day, and women also kept a careful eye on the forest when doing other work in it, such as gathering fuel and medicine. Reversing the degradation of the land was a source of community pride, although not well understood or regarded by the local state.

Everyday encounters with nature and culture also involve building connections and community in different kinds of places too.[8] The effects of austerity, including ongoing job losses in public services are there for all to see in deprived areas of Glasgow. Configured alongside are the community gardens that are sources of social empowerment that energise local people. They work to reclaim derelict land in a deindustrialised city, they involve recent migrants and refugees, and they create jobs in a small way and offer a means of collaborative self-help. They give people the satisfaction of seeing things grow. This kind of phenomenon is easy to dismiss as too little, too late, too specific, but it's precisely in specific actions that alternatives to exploitation get imagined and take shape. Instead of heroes who will rescue us from disaster with their right answers or magic pills, micropolitical practices in ordinary spaces matter. Having said that, there is a technocratic response to environmental crisis that must be looked at.

Green jobs?

Quite a lot of work involves encountering nature. But nature has been recruited to ethical discussions about environmental, social and economic crises in specific ways, via the idea of green jobs – as a way of organising work that reflects the dominance of Question 1 as the route into thinking about work. An enormous range of kinds of work are included, and a range of industries and occupations. The United Nations Environment Programme (UNEP) report on green jobs defines them as: 'positions in agriculture, manufacturing, construction, installation, and maintenance, as well as scientific and technical, administrative, and service-related activities that contribute substantially to preserving or restoring environmental quality'.[9] Most important are paid jobs that protect ecosystems and biodiversity, reduce energy, materials and water consumption, de-carbonise economic activity and minimise waste and pollution. That is to say that 'green work' is that which has a direct and positive impact on nature. This discussion concentrates attention on jobs connected to those sectors most commonly causing environmental degradation (the polluting effects of energy generation, for example).

Notice, however, what is missing: there is no care and little attention to services. The ILO finds this definition narrow, asking what use is green work if it is not decent work? Sociologist David Hess[10] suggests considering a green job as 'employment in a business that engages in some kind of green activity', whether doing a conventional job in a green business, using established skills to reduce environmental impact, or doing a new kind of green work. Kate Crowley differentiates between 'light', 'mid' and 'deep' green work. Deep green work rejects economic growth and works towards ecological sustainability; mid-green work is inspired by 'ecological modernisation' to make existing industry less environmentally damaging; light green jobs are 'afterthoughts that are created by cleaning up and rehabilitating the mess we have made of the environment'.[11] Typologies of intensity focus on defining specific jobs, not on considering the interconnections between kinds of work (for example, jobs induced by a green job).

Disputes over definition contribute to the unsurprising but disappointing absence of data on green jobs. The ILO is still working out how to measure green jobs effectively, discussing what counts as a green job, how to think about job loss as a result of greening and about the skill implications for green work. It faces the challenge of poor quality data and of making reasonable comparisons between places. Academic studies have spent more time forecasting for the future of green jobs than measuring the present. All the data I have seen is made up of estimates from a narrow range of countries. So if you read that around 2.3 million workers are employed in the renewables sector, around half of whom work in (ecologically suspect) biomass,[12] or that of the 235,000 workers manufacturing green vehicles, over half work in the EU,[13] you could reasonably be suspicious of the numbers, not because of any malicious intent, but because the numbers are hard to get. These are likely to be underestimates.

Definitional games are not much fun, though, when the quest for an acceptable definition ends up excluding exactly the complexities that need to be thought about. I prefer to say that 'here are some things to think about when thinking about green work'. One is the interconnections between different kinds of work, and the interconnections across space. Interconnected elements of GPNs have contradictory effects.[14] Renewable energy production or waste recycling may generate new kinds of occupations (for example, energy auditors), which enhance the greenness of existing occupations, while simultaneously relying on geographically distant forms of decidedly non-green work, such as the production of the photovoltaic cells needed by solar panels. A second is the way that how and where debates about what constitutes green work happen tells us a lot about how environmental damage is recruited as a matter of concern and is given an ethics. In the mid-20th century, environmental protection and conservation were assumed to be opposed to market principles. You couldn't protect the environment and push for growth, and growth was more desirable despite the claims of the environmental movement. From some angles, it seems now that the overwhelming desire for economic growth has been reconciled with environmental protection. Ecological modernisation, for example, accepts the reality of climate change (always the privileged environmental crisis) but promises business as usual: economic growth with the threat of environmental catastrophe tidied away.

Current policy-level discussions of greening work are caught up in this 'business as usual' assumption. In the audience at the 2017 EU Green Week, where the theme was green jobs, I heard a senior EU officer who was talking about green jobs say, 'There are 50 shades of green. It doesn't matter what the shade, it's just the general direction.' That's a reference to the discussions in environmental politics and sustainable development about light green and dark green environmental shifts mentioned earlier. A range of more-or-less interchangeable initiatives – greening the economy, the 'circular economy', sustainable development – have been in and out of fashion. I've seen this described as a 'double dividend' (more skilled, decent 'green-collar' jobs that will repair damaged environments and avoid causing further destruction), and as a 'triple win' that means environmental, economic and social objectives will be met through innovation. The circular economy, for example, is a magical promise based on closing the loop of extraction, production, consumption and recycling, by designing out waste, by enabling repair, or by making use of waste. It sounds like a virtuous circle, where innovation and technological change has a positive effect on economic restructuring and will create new jobs. Beyond policy dreams, though, there are issues to discuss about who gains and loses from greening jobs.

Greening unions, greening jobs

Job loss is always contested. In the US (especially in the union movement), being green is often framed, pretty simplistically as 'Jobs Versus the Environment', an encounter that has powerful resonance in particular times and places, for example, when plant closures are on the cards. Much of the discussion about 'green jobs' assumes that the work that counts is heavy work in energy, construction and manufacturing,[15] that is, the loss of men's jobs is the concern. Unions have sometimes argued against green production processes,[16] for example. Other encounters are possible, however, and there are many notable union movements to support the 'just transition' to an environmentally sustainable future that protects workers.[17]

One of the few case studies into greening manufacturing looks at car production. Don't laugh, even if the contradictions of greening a polluting technology might seem a bit out of place. As the discussion of Lars Henriksson in Chapter One showed, contradictions are important to foreground, not to deny. Caleb Goods,[18] in a study of Australian car manufacture and the struggle over green jobs, at least draws attention to the intricate imbecilities of a greened economy and its effect on work. The manufacturers that he studied wanted to produce greener cars – hybrids, electrics and what not. Half of the environmental damage caused by a car over its lifespan is produced during manufacture, however, and so production methods matter as much as what is produced. Goods is not especially interested in relations beyond workplaces, such as thinking about connections with consumerist car culture. He is interested in how trade union response to green initiatives affect how such initiatives are adopted, and points to ways in which green discourses and green values can affect how work is organised. So the question becomes what factors affect trade unions' (different) sensitivities to environmental degradation, and what the interconnections are between green and non-green jobs, and between good green jobs and poor ones. Environmental changes, usually seen as external to bargaining, will be increasingly part of employment relations bargaining and agreements, and part of workplace environmental actions such as supporting sustainable design or greening workplaces.

As well as conflict, though, greening work can be a rare point of agreement for policy-makers, corporate interests, labour unions and community groups.[19] Good green jobs seem like a solution to many, interwoven crises (of energy production, of climate change, of pollution and poisoning of places, and of job loss and job quality). They are the sticking point around which coalitions are built, however unstable. They are boundary objects that entangle different actors: each thinks of the green job in different ways, but shares enough understanding to find compromise. After so many years of only reading about US labour as a problem to be dealt with by attacking its power bases through, for example, legislation that makes collective bargaining hard, reduces the right to strike, and that encourages precarious employment contracts, it is surprising to see labour talked about as a boundary object through which environmental change and economic growth can be achieved. Green work became a frame for agreement between all kinds of actors, including unions and community groups, around which other changes could be put in place. Of course there are other processes getting in on the act, to technology and to corporate understanding of the green sector, which are important, including investment in green tech (by venture capital and other financial institutions) and big corporations developing greening strategies.[20] Corporations, for example, justify moving towards 'green' manufacturing on arguments about economic efficiency – using fewer resources is economically and environmentally good.

The hidden work of infrastructures

Ecological crises have destabilised previously secure jobs in polluting industries. This is most obviously seen in energy production – the biggest challenge faced by models of the sustainable/green/circular economy – as it is essential for a light green transition and its absence might force a deep green transition. The implications of moving away from fossil fuels and towards other energy sources in the US are extensive: new infrastructure, new buildings, new forms of energy extraction – as well as changes to energy use. States and local areas that have moved towards sustainable energy production are more likely to be those where there are not big fossil fuel industries. Arguments for and against new energy production are made in relation to job loss and job creation. This analysis points to the intricacy, contingency and compromise involved in changing energy policy. Some green energy policies also think about social effects, about environmental justice and about job creation in low-income areas. Others follow neoliberal urges to strengthen large corporations; there are even some places that have pushed towards public ownership.[21] Green energy work does not follow a straightforward trajectory.

The costs and damages of extraction (whether for energy production, coal, oil and gas; or for the metals and minerals taken for granted in industrial production for mass consumption – for example, bauxite for aluminium, or cobalt for phones) show some of the problems and compromises that capture the capacity to think about what is to be done in response to environmental crisis. Many green occupations that mitigate environmental damage do not meet decent work criteria.[22] Green industries may treat workers badly. Renewable energy production relies on dangerous and dirty work to extract precious chemicals and metals that make solar panels. Child labour is used in some mineral mining. When it seems that every move towards doing something better involves doing something else that's bad, it's easy to see how inertia and powerlessness emerge, and it can reinforce the feeling that There Is No Alternative.

In addition to thinking about energy production, energy use is also key to thinking about the effect of work on environment. Many corporations have green office policies, and the cynical among us will consider these greenwashing. After all, turning off the lights cuts energy costs for the employer as well as reducing energy use. These micro changes – discouraging printing emails, for example – tend to extend arguments commonly made in relation to consumers to workers: they stress personal responsibility. And while they do change what it is to do work, the changes seem small. Again, there is a link to the discussion in Chapter Seven that is worth articulating, about what the promise of computer technology offers versus what it delivers. The paperless office is considered to be environmentally friendly as well as 'more efficient', but replacing paper with electronic documents stored in the cloud just hides the energy use. A Google server farm needs the equivalent power to operate as does Honolulu.[23] I'm not sure why Honolulu, or whether that's going to catch on as a unit of comparison. But both technology design and assumptions that technological solutions are better, greener solutions have to be unpacked more carefully, alongside other parts of economic and social life that are commonly hidden. Of those, waste is especially important.

A highly technologised 'digital' world relies on plastic.[24] The computers that generate the global flows of data on which so much of current economic activity depends (the links between EPOS tills, logistics and manufacturing, for example), are plastic. And plastic, a product of the oil industry, is long lasting, to put it mildly. Disposing of such machines, parts of which are toxic and parts of which are valuable, is a complicated process involving global movements. Indeed, some of the container ships that take consumer goods from China to the US return with e-waste. Extracting precious metals from e-waste is dirty and dangerous and damages workers' health,[25] and it is exported out of view of consumers. Hazardous waste that gets classed as recyclable can be exempt from laws controlling toxic waste, making it even more dangerous to work on.

Waste

All kinds of waste, not just that produced by consumers, have environmental and economic implications, and thinking about waste tells us a lot about the knotty problem of environment and work. Some corporations have introduced campaigns against waste and landfill, often as part of corporate social responsibility. Reducing waste in production and packaging is one of those triple wins: cut costs, improve brand value and control the supply chain. It's a competitive response to a real threat. It's rare, however, for the impact of this kind of process on work to be properly considered. The 'circular economy' brings a new attitude to waste. It seems to close the loop, so that waste stops being, well, wasted, and becomes valuable. What's not to like? What that means is that recycling and reuse becomes not the added extra activity of a virtuous citizen, but a whole source of financial exchange.

Recycling is a way of getting consumers to put work into reducing their power over the environment. It is common practice, encouraged by state and local policy through both nudging consumers/residents and by designing recycling structures. Consumer waste from within households might be sorted, washed, reused or transported elsewhere. Relationships within households affect that work, as do local systems for managing waste: do local authorities collect waste?[26] Can informal workers make small amounts of money from collecting waste plastic? The hidden labour of plastic recycling in Ghana is a result of neoliberal governmental policies that encourage consumption of water in bottles, as a substitute for investing in improving supplies of running water.[27] We see here how informal economic activities (done mostly by women, mostly older people, mostly migrants) are affected by government policies and how they are connected to formal economy (plastic pickers sell by weight to a middleman who sells on to a formally registered waste treatment plant). Recycling work takes a different form where 'waste' materials are transformed by women working in cooperatives in the Philippines into home accessories or jewellery for sale in global markets.[28] Products are marketed to consumers as ecologically and socially ethical, and recycling thereby seems like one of those virtuous circles: a sensitive consumer can buy well. It's even possible that the very promise that something can be recycled makes it seems disposable in the first place.

There seem to be a few simple solutions to the problem of waste. Re-use and refurbishment delays disposal, and it isn't that straightforward. A non-profit organisation that trained people to repair old computers struggled to sell on the products they got working again. The organisation was sustained through government funding; there was no market for either the products they got working again, nor paid work for those with the skills to mend them. In contrast, a private sector organisation didn't bother with refurbishment, as they couldn't make any profit. They removed data (people will pay for that) and employed migrant workers on a disassembly line to strip out the most valuable metals and minerals. This is hazardous work. There is a real difference between the high-level technical skills that greening the economy is supposed to deliver, and the low-level skills actually being used, which, when added to the small numbers of people needed to do this recycling work, make the promises of new, decent, green work pretty hard to believe in.[29]

Recycling work involves heat, dirt and danger – this is the case for the ship breaker yards in Bangladesh[30] and for waste management and resource recovery in Europe.[31] In Europe it is likely to be done by migrant workers, often from elsewhere in the EU. Local workers reject the low skilled and physically dirty work as tainted; the largely Polish, Turkish or Czech migrant workers valorise themselves by thinking of the work as risky. This is not unusual: most migrant workers in Europe end up in sectors that aren't readily outsourced to the Global South but are deregulated and rely on cheap labour.[32] Construction, agriculture and services make use of informal contracts. Once again, Pajnik's description of the work as 3D (Dirty, Dangerous and Demanding) is apt.[33] For the poorest of waste pickers, actually doing recycling work is a problem. It is especially dangerous for those who can only afford the most basic equipment – perhaps using acids to leach metals from circuit boards.[34]

Recycling can only be a solution to environmental crisis if (hidden) work is put in place to make it happen. As mentioned, waste work is rarely good work. In the US, prison labourers used old technologies. This is forced labour, racialised because of the racial inequalities for which the US prison system is infamous. Other places used privatised waste management firms. Waste contractors make money in two ways. One is by selling on the waste goods – or at least the valuable parts of them (metals, and rare metals and minerals from electronics equipment, having especially thriving markets). The other is to do what subcontractors usually do: cut costs by paying workers less and making conditions worse. Waste supply chains rely on informal workers who get incorporated into global value chains in the worst possible way. First, they do bad work for minimal reward. Second, waste management subcontracting removes opportunities for waste picking to be a short-term survival strategy in the grey economy. It gets formalised beyond the reach of people who, while they might certainly not want to choose waste picking, would rather do so on their own account, scavenging in order to sell valuables on, than under the whip of a gangmaster. That is, waste stops being a common resource and becomes part of corporate value chain. Formalisation perpetuates worker vulnerability.[35]

Environmental expertise

In Nepal, geographically distant conservation experts in the district forest office began to influence high caste men in a community that had long engaged closely with the forest. The men tried to restrict women from gathering the leaf litter that was used as fertiliser in smallholdings. Ecological science considers this damaging work. Women resisted the new rules from outside by making use of established community values about gendered division of labour and about ritual pollution to refuse to stop collecting.[36] In these kinds of technocratic solutions to economic/environmental disaster, expertises are assembled in order to locate solutions. But solutions often bring different problems.

Work makes the world when expertise defines and circumscribes acceptable knowledge. In The World Bank, biodiversity, conservation and other ecological concepts and practices are cemented into regulatory regimes that are then embedded in investment programmes designed by World Bank professionals, generally a cadre of consultants based in, or trained in the Global North.[37] The programmes are strategies to govern populations living in resource-rich (if economically poor) areas. People living in these areas are seen as objects of concern, as not modern enough. They do small-scale production – agriculture, fishing, foraging. Despite relying on sophisticated knowledge, including of the habits and tendencies of nature, this is seen as backwards. Around 2000, environmental NGOs began to be contracted by The World Bank to do feasibility studies for environmentally significant developments (for example, dams). This meant that their organisational function and position changed. From being critics, they became 'stakeholders'; feasibility studies follow parameters that make critical insights difficult: The World Bank, which wants to invest in development projects, has little interest in funding feasibility studies that say 'No'. In some instances feasibility reports were reshaped, with negative findings omitted or simplified conclusions drawn from nuanced evidence.[38] Affected populations might be consulted, but their voices tended to be silenced (can they even be heard by those who speak the language of economic development?). In this story, one element of the relationship between politics and how work is organised is on show, through The World Bank's assumptions that progress means the end of established ways of making a living and engaging with the environment. There are other ways in which we can think about how science (an assemblage that includes scientists) comes to know 'the environment', and to offer technological remedies. Scientists with different specialisms, policy-makers, NGO workers and other knowledge workers are part of the epistemic communities on whose work and beliefs others rely. Senior environmental policy-makers from four European states reveal a more interesting tension between professionalism, expertise and 'subjective values'.[39] Advisors held strong personal commitments to ecological values, but policies rarely acknowledged that values might be important, using economic justifications presented in abstract, social-scientific language. It is an indicator of how economy-first thinking writes out other ethical issues that matter.

Sometimes the effects of environmental policy-making are problematic. Regulations that exist in relation to the environment have weak effects because the objects being regulated are unpredictable. Ecological change isn't steady and consistent. It's affected by sudden events: oil spills, floods, bad winters and dry summers. It varies immensely between places. There are no simple equilibria. With this in mind, a couple of ecologists[40] comment on the stupidities (my word) of command and control ecologies. Simply applying regulations agreed elsewhere and set down in bullet points generates ecological problems. That's because specific places are shaped in time and space, and don't conform to the assumptions on which the regulations rely. I make sense of their advice to avoid 'prescriptions and cookbook approaches'[41] using the ideas of skilled bodies and craft work (Chapter Four), as it indicates to me the importance of local and specific responses to observed changes, of regularly sensing and judging what is needed, and of having the chance to respond suitably. It therefore indicates the importance of care at the point of doing work, rather than the application of standardised judgement. Regulation relies on the assumption that what is to be regulated can be adequately captured. But regulations regularly fail to understand settings, and disputes over how to understand settings are common.

Environmental science as work

Scientific expertise, itself a form of labour, plays a critical role in providing insights into environmental degradation and its solutions. Global warming – sometimes disputed by those who are funded or persuaded by oil companies and others resistant to economic reforms – is a clear example of a problem identified by science as a cause for concern, and that requires a response by citizens and policy-makers. Environmental concern and activity (mediated by science) has an impact, then, on the constitution of work (as green work, or as damaging and destructive work).

Greening the economy involves an enormous change to socio-technological systems.[42] Energy production, building design and use, transport, the organisation of all industrial sectors, the management of consumption and disposal are all involved in such a change. Changes are slow and unpredictable, and vulnerable to the kinds of technological-saviour hype seen in Chapter Seven. Cold, distant neutrality in the face of environmental change characterises some scientific responses. Neutral science lays claim to provide technological solutions to environmental change, while ignoring the vulnerabilities of others. Environmental management is inspired by scientisation and securitisation more than protection and healing.[43] Longstanding, if contradictory, military interest in environmental concerns is shown when wealthy governments look to securing water, energy and borders. The US military engagement in 'environmental compliance' for example, cleaning radioactive waste from the landscape, is one such example.[44] Here are work practices that seem to engender sustainability but that produce more social divisions, more pollution.

Geoengineering (the deliberate manipulation of climate to ameliorate the effects of climate change), for example, is posited as an environmental 'solution' by (predominantly male) US-based scientists who understand science as power over nature and who valorise technological competence over awareness of the social effects of technology.[45] Stengers, always worried by promises of cures, speaks of geoengineering as 'at the stage of fiction, but we know that soon this fiction will be proposed, and will try to impose itself, as the only "logical" solution, whether we like it or not'.[46]

Different sciences operate in different ways, with different questions, different assemblages. A field experiment to trace the effect of GMO corn pollen falling on monarch butterflies' food looked at two kinds of scientists: geneticists (working for biotech) and ecologists (working for butterflies).[47] They developed a politically significant contest over ethics and the nature of science during the experiment. Different knowledges, tacit assumptions, politics and values are present in such contests. It's not always easy to tell what these are: ecologists' published scientific papers rarely indicate that conservation matters and are more likely to say that curiosity is the motive for ecological research. I think there are two things going on there. First, that science defends itself through a claim to curiosity, as curiosity is an acceptable feeling with no apparent politics to it. It is therefore okay to admit to it in a published paper. Second, that fear of being worthy, the power of the judgement of piety, can make people reluctant to say what matters to them. It's hard to talk about doing good in a cynical world that is caught up in the 'business as usual' mentality of 'There Is No Alternative'. I make this second observation because of research I have done with environmental consultants, where some of these complexities and uncertainties are on show (alongside other things too).

In my research into environmental labour, I've thought about how careful and caring work is engendered by particular kinds of flows of feeling and ethical commitments. Engagement with elements of the natural world – gorillas, orchids and Japanese knotweed are among the more exciting sources that generate business opportunities – push people into careers, inform their decisions about training and education, about work that they consider worthwhile.[48] Care for nature is caught up in the web of other social, cultural and – crucially – economic relations. Hippies and vegetarians are economic actors too, and dualist ethical reasoning isn't helpful (it's not that environmental consultants must choose either the airport or the protected species, it is that there are layers of relationships, feelings and possibilities to be worked through). Didier Fassin's ideas[49] (Chapter One) encourage thinking about how ethical subjectivities are framed within institutional formations. Environmental consultants really act in the world, through the decisions they make and the negotiations they have with airport authorities. They might be sensitive to not preaching or being pious, because that puts off the people they are trying to persuade, even as they hold strong beliefs about cushioning the effects of environmental damage. This work involves managing tensions between economic and ecological valuations, as when different kinds of scientific, technocratic and local (indigenous) knowledges encounter each other and the earth.

Most of the environmental consultants I've interviewed work in small businesses and are contracted to do studies by bigger organisations, corporations and sometimes non-profit agencies, including state agencies, who outsource this kind of specialised work. This is dirty science in two ways. It literally encounters dirt, and it figuratively works with ethically complex operations to enforce local, national and super-national eco- and wildlife regulations. Consultants have worked on projects they hated, like checking to see if property developers have met wildlife protection regulations, and others they have felt an emotional connection to, like moorland restoration. They have negotiated with others in their business about how to work, and how to play the game, and sat in long meetings with clients to persuade them to make changes.

Environmental consultancy, therefore, is a series of negotiations that capture and create feelings. It has many grey areas that require ethical compromises between the assembled actors. Entanglements of personal ethics, natures, affects and imperatives, and of science and credentialised knowledge are significant to economic activity. Economic activity is a lived engagement in the lively materiality of natures, and environmental activity is constrained by, but not reducible to, the lively, material and discursive power of economy. This assemblage means that there are many moments of pragmatic compromise between human and corporate actors with their different interests, and with the science and possibility of what could be done to the woodland or moorland area. The negotiations constitute what can and does happen, in non-linear ways. The future matters, though it is somewhat nebulous; more important are the possibilities offered by the present.

The possibilities of the present

The degradation of the environment, indicated by pollution and climate change, plus persistently unequal global development attached to stagnant growth, precarious work and overconsumption seems to find an easy solution in new policies to 'green' the economy, or make the economy 'sustainable'. This tells us something about the complex relationship between ecological sustainability, modernity and economic development that I talked about earlier. Consultants' work both redefines economic growth (for example, by showing the costs of growth), and enhances it (for example, in enabling developments to take place within regulatory guidelines). Any consultancy may reject and reinvent elements of, say, a development plan, and create a compromise between key actors. Here is a conundrum then: globalised economic development and 'modernisation' can degrade the environment, and can also produce policies and practices that will ameliorate these effects. Environmental solutions cast social shadows,[50] as in the case of job loss in energy production, or the dirty and dangerous work of dealing with waste.

Within the apparent monolith of capitalism are pockets of alternatives: economic relationships (via work) that involve commitment to making good on environmental damage. These are sometimes co-opted into a business as usual mentality. They are rarely deep green; they are not reducible to anti-capitalist protest either. They are easily described as too little, too pious, too unrealistic. I do think it really matters that people want to make the world better. Are people really only interested in their own lives? If not, then the tone and nature of discussions about the kinds of power people have, including workers, really affects what might happen. The coming barbarism is based on the idea that people are uninterested and content to let the world be decided for them.

NINE

Biting back

Asking questions about good and bad work

There have been many, many books written to answer the question of what good work is and what bad work is. Studying work always involves making normative claims about what is wrong with work. How questions get asked affects the route to finding possible solutions. So where the question is 'How does exploitation happen?' and the answer is through the alienation of a homogeneous class of workers, then possible solutions are radical class-based transformation. This kind of reasoning and political thinking is both powerful and important, but also limited. It underplays spatial and temporal differences between people, singularities become generalities and some kinds of work get ignored. Where the question is 'What is good work?', answers refer to fairness at work, meaningful work, dignity at work, even the pleasures of a work ethic. These bring forward thoughts about work being better when it develops individual capabilities, when it offers self-fulfilment as well as material benefits. Bad work is exploitative, not offering enough material and/or social benefits – such as adequate pay and recognition – and risking damage to workers' health. Much commentary on good work draws on ideas from the ethics of justice, especially ideas around autonomous individuals. Ethical claims have pragmatic effects; justice ethics (and care ethics) have pragmatic value in calling some things into notice, and I do not want to throw that away. But nor can it be that there is one right way to think about the ethics and politics of work. Think in terms of care and the ethics of care, and relationality through work comes to the fore.

In the course of this book, I have encountered much that it is hard to be against – universal ethics, dignity at work, bullet point lists as to what makes good and bad work. But I am still not certain that easy solutions can be found to the problem of what is wrong with work, because so many of the ideas that are used to think about work tend to be abstract and generalised, unwilling to address the complexity of differentiation, with a strong preference instead for critical distancing and/or regulations. Debating good work and bad work is important, but 'What is a good job and what is a bad job?' is not the right question for me. It flattens out differences of gender, class, race, migration status and place. It removes the insight into work from its relationship to catastrophic present and future times where environmental degradation creates a struggle to live, where economic exploitation makes everyday survival hard, and where the social effects of technological change are treated as inevitable.

I've asked what's wrong with work. It seems obvious that the answer can't be limited to the question of how workers are treated. Imagine that you work in a factory producing agrochemicals. The work is dangerous to you; you inhale toxic air, your protective safety gear is old and worn, and anyway, some of the people with whom you work think that safety gear isn't manly. Your work damages you and your workmates. It pollutes the town around you. The rivers are dirty and the air is heavy. The capitalocentric explanation for this is that it is capitalism doing its thing: damaging workers and not compensating them enough, damaging the local environment. That's a fine explanation as far as it goes. It doesn't go very far, though. Solutions are often bifurcated: protect the environment, but risk jobs; protect jobs, but risk the environment. Answers based around 'Jobs Versus the Environment' aren't enough. They don't recognise the interconnections of work, the care work that the poisonous factory generates, for example. Answers based on 'it's capitalism' get to only part of the story. They underplay the interweaving of, say, demand for chemicals, management decisions not to replace safety equipment, scientists' misreadings of risk, a momentary mistake by a colleague, a machine that hasn't been mended properly, and so on. The ethics they foreground is one of judgement and blame, not of foresight and care.

The connected elements of economic, environmental, technological and everyday life crises relate to the connections between kinds of work. This tells me that it's impossible to say that the only ethics that matters is the ethics of how workers are treated – even as that is impossible to ignore. Instead of taking the practice of work for granted we should study what it does and how it does it. Instead of abstracting into categories (of low, medium, high skilled; of good or bad; of clean and dirty work), we should think more precisely about what is involved in doing work.

My questions

'What's wrong with work?' is a question without an easy answer. It has a resonance in daily life, as when we complain to our friends about our day, or when we join in with collective political activities, as well as in the technocratic management of work through regulations and rights. And, of course, corporations, managers, employees, own account workers and the silent mass of domestic carers across the world are among those who might have a great deal to say in answer to the question.

The issues raised by asking what's wrong with factory work aren't the same as the questions raised by other kinds of work. Assumptions create narrow answers and limited solutions. By shifting the focus through a series of extra assumptions and questions and alternative concepts, I made a different kind of discussion. I don't think that it's possible to develop a clear insight into work without undeleting some of the work that matters, adding in care work and service work and recognising the gendering and racialisation of these activities. Care work is a clear reminder that work has an effect on the world as well as on the life of the worker.

In order to keep the door open to allow a more extensive answer to the question of what's wrong with work to enter, I have been asking myself three, interrelated questions. Question 1 is: How is work organised? Question 2 is: How are different kinds of work interconnected? And Question 3 is: What does work do? Question 1 tends to dominate many accounts of work. From it flow many questions concerning ethics and fairness. These include: Is pay/compensation a fair reflection of the skill or effort needed (is skill even seen)? And this in turn leads to questions about the social factors that influence how something is or isn't thought of as a skill (status, gender, equality are important). There are many ways of organising work, and the ethical questions raised by them are not reducible to the ethics of fair pay in waged work, nor to the issues of the conditions of employment. Questions 2 and 3, however, quickly emerge as part of the understanding that we can start to develop. Exemplary figures of global production networks – logistics workers (ship workers), garment makers or brand agents – are dependent on each other despite being geographically dispersed. Distant damage and distant caring raise their heads as the control and organisation of work is contingent, negotiated and full of human feeling.

Care work explodes the assumption that the only work that should count (that deserves our attention) is waged work. Care work is organised in many different ways and different kinds of care work exist simultaneously – and there is cultural variation in any 'typical' way of organising care. It's impossible to understand care work without attending to gender, age, race, migration status as well as class. The vulnerability of bodies generates a whole array of caring work, from that done by medical professionals of many kinds, to the work of cleaning and protecting sick bodies, to the emotional commitments of looking after and caring for others – and each of these might overlap. It is done by paid workers, whether considered highly skilled and educated or low paid and seemingly interchangeable; it is also done extensively by family and community, and it is gendered. It relies on commodes and other commodities bought, borrowed or provided by a welfare state system, on formal and vernacular medicines, and on care services and so on.

The broader spectrum of what counts as work and how that work is organised forces us to raise different questions and ask familiar questions in new ways. In factory work, fair pay and pay equality are well-established arenas for ethical and political debate and activism. In some contexts, though, gratitude, family inheritance, exchange of favours or intergenerational obligations matter, and intimate care relies on global care chains. Care work is not some kind of romantic idyll free of economic relations, full of cooperation, not competition and meeting 'real' needs, not abstract money values.

Work that is not paid is still work; work that is not contracted for but that is still paid is still work. If we pretend that work that is readily made invisible (denied, deleted) doesn't exist, then I admit, it's easier to find solutions to what's wrong with work (largely: better pay, better regulations to treat workers). But it's like painting a wall without moving the furniture. However good a job you do of the visible bits, you've left a lot out. And the chances are that it will be the gendering and racialisation of hidden work that would get missed, along with the effects of what work does to other humans and non-humans in the world. Post-work ideas promise the end of productive paid labour. I find it impossible to accept these arguments. By not being careful about what gets counted as work, they are not careful about what would come after work.

Repair

The interrelations of work are deep. Examples have been given in other chapters: the design of machines affects the human who uses or repairs it; the care work of cleaning and the care work of being kind are entangled, the management of risk/health and safety executives affects the chance of damage at work and the expert affects the lives of others. Mundane and ordinary practices of doing work are the worthless rock in which ethical issues sit. Work acts in the world. Different kinds of work have radically different kinds of effects in the world, that's clear. Sometimes it is the case that workers know that *how* they work has effects beyond their own experience – this can be where ideas of doing a good job matter, where the link between the personal experience of working, and what that work is doing in the world becomes very important. Doing a job in a slapdash way or to finish it properly affects how long the work lasts for, how others encounter it. Sometimes, there is very little of this kind of effect visible, perhaps because a job has been designed and is managed in a way that sucks out all autonomy and sense of independent effort. Still, thinking about work as doing brings out its active, transforming possibility, its effects on humans and non-humans. The ethical effects of IT work, software work and (relatedly) job design provide examples for thinking about this.

Failures, breakdowns, interruptions, mistakes, foolish decisions and selfish decisions also destabilise, unintentionally. The myth of smooth systems and perfect procedures is one that deserves more attack. From active breakdown comes change. Repair and maintenance are central to work. Failure on the production line; software updates, tweaks and work-arounds; policy reversals, the repair of the broken earth, and of ill people, and of machines that make and do stuff is ordinary: from street cleaners to marketing executives strategising about addressing failing sales. Repair is care, it points to infrastructures. Investigating repair, mundane and hidden, helps to think about how change happens. It helps to counter assumptions about the healing capabilities of technological progress.

The limits of capitalocentric reasoning

Economy theory has a power to affect the world and it takes that power as a right. Sociological theories rarely even think that they are right, let alone assert their power. This is a benefit of sociology because problems can be reframed and potential solutions rethought. Rethinking the problem of work for me has involved moving away from seeing economic activity as a singular, monolithic entity. Monolithic capitalism gives rise to homogenising economy-first explanations of everyday life. That writes out other possibilities, other things that matter. It writes out feeling, other than feelings that are captured by economic processes; it writes out gifts and favours and alternative economic spaces. It makes it much harder to hear the birds singing. It is based on assumptions that accept that economy is its own space, unique, powerful and all-consuming. In so doing, critical voices against capitalism harmonise with the melody lines of pro-market, economic determinists (who otherwise hold very different political views). Capitalism is everywhere, they intone. The performative effects of economic ideas bubble out of the many places in which they dwell, sedimented into policy documents that set political agendas, in management 'best practice' techniques made possible through specific software technologies full of unacknowledged assumptions, as well as in the curricula of MBAs, management advice books from airport stalls and in many layers of professional work and policy-making. Such accoutrements of flexible capitalism, the policies and practices that are commonly, if over-enthusiastically, described as 'neoliberal' – as though it was self-evident what that was – are important forces recruiting humans and non-humans as actors into the production of economic value. But that description is less complete than it pretends; it cannot quite admit the presence of not-capitalism.

The 'race to the bottom' thesis compares the power and mobility of corporations to the vulnerability of labour. That's a race you don't want to win. In a world where corporations move production to where labour is cheapest, advocating for higher wages and better rights is counterproductive. Heads they win, tails we lose. The logic of inevitability – this is just what capital does, no one can resist the force of globalising neoliberalism – is powerful in persuading people not to complain: once again There Is No Alternative. We learn to live with the risk of future precarity, if we aren't already dealing with the experience of current precarity. TINA is a powerful force for removing conflict. And the loss of work does weaken established labour movements. But new low wage workforces can and do generate new and strong labour movements.[1] Capital is not the all-powerful force it seems. A supply chain that uses just-in-time production is more vulnerable to disruption than one that has stockpiled material.[2] Stories of challenge to TINA, differences and unexpected outcomes make it much harder to sustain a fatalistic argument that nothing can ever be different, or better, that capitalism just is.

We've got used to hearing the refrain of TINA about economic decisions that seem to come from an untameable beast that must have blood. But the more we think about how these decisions are made and the conceptualisation of economy that form them, how disembedded they are, and how their politics denies being a politics, then the more scope there is for asking questions about what could be different. Simple understandings of dominant capitalism, glossed as neoliberalism, serve to underplay important elements of the contemporary crises. Summing up widely different practices in shorthand is cheating, because all the answers are already decided in advance. Trying some slow thinking about what counts as part of the problem, the knots of technology, environment and everyday life came into view, and in this book I have been thinking about the ways those lines of thought were entangled together. So new platform technologies of logistics and control make for different ways of organising everyday service provision; care provisions are restructured by market operations, but also by the way different phenomena are called into concern as worthy of care, whether care for a damaged environment or lack of care for a distant stranger. Long, long, troubling histories of exploitation re-emerge in the present as environmental damage and perilous livelihoods. Technology, nature, or fluid social life don't sprout out of economic discourse and practice; their effects are diffuse and complicated. I bear this in mind as I again ask the question 'What's wrong with work?'

The scope of expertise, its particularity, experts' sense of what knowledge is (scientism, community practices, listening or hearing) and their sense of what constitutes an improvement to the world (a new HR policy, more regulations) is significant. This is a moral worldview where the experts' own work makes realities through the words they use and the actions that produce the world. The ethical effects of expert work are seen when a job is designed to be 'bad work' because those involved in its design do not value the people who will be doing the work as much as they value other attributes – the desire is to reduce costs, especially labour costs, often justified by understandings of the legitimacy of particular kinds of neoliberal economic reasoning. The ethical effects of what a form of work does to the world are real and important and not reducible to how work is organised.

Governance and standards

One of the possible routes for making changes and removing unacceptable work is through the application of standards and regulations, ideally backed up by legal enforcement. There are many kinds of campaigns, regulations and strategies operating at the level of global governance. 'Decent work' is the umbrella concept for improving work that comes out of the ILO, a compromise that relies on agreements between states, employers and unions. It is vague partly because it is a compromise between actors with different interests, and because it covers the enormous complexity of work, including the very many forms taken by informal work. The ILO promotes 'opportunities for women and men to obtain decent and productive work, in conditions of freedom, equality, security and human dignity'[3] through promoting principles of rights at work, employment, social protection and social dialogue. It is impossible to say that these considerations are wrong. And yet, partly because the ILO has no power to enforce, only to promote, it's not exactly clear what the power and effect of these principles are.

Companies sign up to voluntary codes (or create their own) and police their own adherence to them. These corporate social responsibility (CSR) strategies are, in the most cynical view, mere window-dressing to disguise the hidden exploitations, and, in the most positive view, the reasonable actions of apparently caring capitalism. Global Framework Agreements (GFA), negotiated between large companies and a broad range of trade unions (covering different geographical spaces and different industries and occupations), are one attempt to develop a strategy with more teeth, reflecting that part of the decent work agenda that is about enhancing social dialogue. GFAs specify that all elements of a supply chain should cover minimum standards for workers, such as no use of child labour, adherence to decent work, no use of unfree work. Nothing wrong with the idea at all, even if employers resist and prefer to tout voluntary initiatives,[4] and mid-level managers tend not to know or understand them.[5]

Much of the discussion about global standards and the 'race to the bottom' focuses on managing and curbing transnational corporations (TNCs), as being most likely to be pressured into signing up to codes of conduct and monitoring suppliers. But when even suppliers themselves complain about the behaviour of TNCs forcing them to 'green' production methods while refusing to pay extra for the suppliers' products, the limits of such standards are clearly on show.[6] Codes and monitoring do indeed look an awful lot like window-dressing, especially where auditors are few and under-trained.[7] Economic downturns in the Global North have a notable impact on worker safety in the Global South[8] when managers make 'tough decisions' to cut costs by demanding reductions in the price from suppliers or cutting 'nonessential programmes' such as CSR.

Other modes of governance do excellent work in assessing bad work. Models of unacceptable forms of work below the minimum range of decent work,[9] models and measurements of job quality,[10] and of 'good jobs',[11] as well as the modelling and measurements of precarious work (Chapter Five) are all commendable, in the sense that they struggle with the enormous problem of finding good ways to think about the prevalence of bad work. In generating forms of comparison and measurement, against which specific work can be assessed, the typologies that emerge from this work do excellent service in the terms they set for themselves. However, they are troubling to me in two ways. First, making models involves making selections of criteria to include and exclude which can then be applied to the world. That's not wrong in itself, but it's not all that can be done. The application of objective criteria gets to be like stargazing without a telescope. Some constellations are visible, but quite a lot is beyond the naked eye. But the 'truth' of the criteria – the rightness of the measure – ends up reified as the *right* way to think about good work. I prefer a reasoned openness that attends to variability and specificity and that is cautious about what it feels it can claim. That inevitably means that claims are more tenuous, and accepting indeterminacy has losses as well as gains. Second, that the issue of what happens next isn't clear. It is not that it is reasonable to expect that the expert work that makes and measures models is also the expert work that seeks to change how work is organised (although that does sometimes go together). It is that the technocratic expert systems, the big global organisations, don't enact change.

Remembering Stengers (Chapter One), it seems to me that these strategies are examples of the logical solutions and techno-fixes that self-appointed Guardians tend to offer (and succeed in imposing through the feeling of the infernal alternative). Global governance through the actions of civil services, policy, regulations, legal status, enforcement in nation-states; of transnational institutions like The World Bank, EU or ILO – all differing in the edge they bring and the teeth they've got to bite with; NGOs; and the multifaceted corporations in multiple sectors are all actors with obvious power. Governance and techno-fixes shift conflict over how to live into the rarefied atmospheres inhabited by those who know best. And regulations can become technologies of control, not ethical commitments.[12] The Play Fair campaign shows that the health and safety legislation that is intended to protect workers from physical risks gets ignored in some places because the journey from regulation to application hasn't been thought about.[13] The damages that result are easily hidden. Few speak about the injuries experienced by those who built sports stadia while the competition is on. Those same regulations, however, emerge as a technique of political control on the odd occasions when it is politically desirable to notice damage to workers' bodies, for example, when making judgements about which nations are 'Human Rights abusers'. Sorry, there is no alternative: regulations are slippery beasts.

In *The Man with the Golden Gun*, James Bond is in a hall of mirrors shooting at things that merely look like they can be killed off with a bullet. A new list of morals and standards to shoot at is not what is needed, for these are unduly fixed and hold imaginations hostage. A shift in ethics-as-ethos in the structures of feeling around possibility might energise the bite back, the conditions of possible action. That means hearing what existing movements there are, already biting back. I do not think that people are agents of neoliberal society, atomised with no sense of others. Getting over Stockholm syndrome means rethinking the sense of capture and impossibility. Yes, governance could be more careful and more humble. But it might be better if democracy could bubble up, and a new conversation about economic redistribution emerges.[14]

Bubble up responses

'Common sense' about solutions tends to support the interests of Guardians of capital. The global decline of trade unionisation has been an important factor in the flexibilisation of work and the persistently poor treatment of many workers. It has also resulted in fewer opportunities for public conversation about what constitutes good work. That is on display when right-wing media analysis of union activities tends to present any industrial action as an attack on or problem for consumers. These kinds of media campaigns try to leverage conflict and envy, asking citizens to ignore the rights of others to decent work and to ignore their own interests as workers in order to see the rights of others to strike as illegitimate. When called to take an ethical position as 'consumer', what if we tried to hear ourselves as being called 'workers'?

It seems intensely reasonable that people should have the right to organise to campaign for their own interests, to be part of setting rules and regulations and generating norms and values. The power and activity of trade unions is variable, whether because of legislative restrictions on what unions can do, or unions' own reluctance to recognise some kinds of invisible workers as important, or where employing organisations refuse to permit unionisation. (Sometimes this is done by an organisation offering 'family'-style relationships and the use of internal processes that delegitimise complaints; others encourage workers to identify closely with the organisation, profession or sector.)

Traditional trade unions have sometimes been reluctant to engage with precarious workers or informal work, choosing to protect established interests. Occupational, ethnic and gender divisions can create in- and out-groups. Campaigns around movements (for minimum wages, for a living wage) can and have subverted those tendencies, as in the case of the low-paid, precarious, outsourced, immigrant and women of colour working in Canada as cleaners in health services.[15] That is often, but not always, overlaid with ideas about male breadwinner wages and interests being more important than women's work, and involves perpetuating inequalities of gender, race, class and migration status through work. However, some unions have responded to the interests of informal workers, especially those involved in outsourced production. And there are other instances of self-organising (migrant care workers being again the easy example to turn to). Institutional changes get driven from below. In the #schedulesthatwork campaign, service workers organised so as to be less vulnerable to zero hours contracts; similarly, when farm workers bypass direct employers to talk to big buyers,[16] or when homeworkers collaborate to negotiate new piece rates, then change bubbles up from the actions of workers. These re-positionings are a tiny response to the blandishments of Guardians who know best.

The ethics and politics of work isn't just a question of how to think about our own work, although that really matters. One implication is to think about the work we encounter, done by others, for example, fair trade that asks the consumer to think; fast fashion that requires forgetting the distant other. Work that involves a politics of citizenship, as when migration politics are tied to work or state benefit policies that are linked to the promotion of workfare, and it invokes an ethics of empathy – with the risk of imposing the right to care on those who might not want your care. Ethical consumption, while not a substitute for other modes of articulating decent work, is a place to think about work. NGO worker rights campaigns (Clean Clothes and so on) draw on the power of consumer voices to shame organisations for dreadful employment practices. Rana Plaza, however, is a clear indication of the limits of this kind of work. Only some of the big BGR companies who used Rana Plaza contributed to the restitution fund; only some stopped using sweatshop production. Other consumer-related campaigns are also contentious and ambiguous. Fairtrade, and other accreditation organisations, which aim to guarantee raw-material producers a reasonable income in return for a kitemark to show consumers that ethical standards are met has been criticised for its limitations. Nonetheless, the problems with work should not be thought of as only affecting workers, nor indeed as only something for workers to act on. These are global social problems that require broad attention.

An anti-crisis future

There are many problems with how work is organised in the present, and these are damaging to the lives of workers and the environments in which they live. 'What's wrong with work?' is a question that has to be understood in relation to current crises of environmental disaster, and to the destabilising effects of zombie economic policy, to technological solutionism and to the constant challenge of everyday life. Work has changed and will keep changing. It may (differently, in different places) be intensified, become more precarious, and make use of new technologies. Everyday life is affected by how work activities combine, how they are organised and what they do in the world. Many, many people make claims as to what the future will bring. The future of paid work is said to be automation and a post-work life; the future of human life, however, could be extinction. With no planned exit from quantitative easing in the Global North, financialisation or the privileging of shareholder interest, a future of more economic crisis is plausible. It's easy to focus on the robots coming for jobs, because that seems tangible. It's what sci-fi has been preparing us for. The poisoned planet, a more subtle and insidious threat, looms larger for me. Deep in the thicket it may be, noticeable if you see that rodents don't die off because winters aren't cold enough, perhaps. But it is really present, and it has real present effects. Pretending it doesn't matter, that it won't affect us, is the less scary option, but a foolish one. It is visible to farmers presented with desertification or flooding, to fishing fleets not finding their usual catch, to disaster workers stressed and stretched to get clean drinking water, to women who walk further to get water, to tourist workers in ski resorts with no snow and no visitors, and others going through their daily routines. It's big. What's a person to do with that set of predictions? Crisis and the feeling of end times can easily generate cynicism and hopelessness, and those feelings get in the way of action. Step one is to imagine some different possibilities.

Imagining the future is a strange occupation. If you watch sci-fi films from the 1960s, you see lots of robots, but no remote controls, and no internet. Futurologists offered a world free of work, as machinery would increase productivity and give people more leisure. It didn't turn out like that. Will this time be different? The future won't be what we think it will be, but what could it be? Imaginaries are powerful and any imaginary is also an assertion, sometimes a simple one of unquestionable 'common sense'. So, the imaginary of cyber-capitalism is that IT will work; the imaginary of greening the economy is that nature can be soothed without loss; the imaginary of flexibility is that it is life-affirming and friction free. This kind of common sense, which seems so logical, needs more questioning. And other imaginaries need building, ones that are more questioning of common sense and things we have been told to believe.

Some plans and solutions for the problems of the present imply a particular view of the past. Nostalgia for what work used to be like is common in every era. As part of today's crises stems from political decisions to reduce welfare state support, then nostalgia for the European welfare state compromise of the 1950s and 1960s seems reasonable, as its break down is a real loss for those who benefited. We are aware now that such allocations (of rights and of economic rewards) were narrowly made. Many were excluded from its rewards: most obviously those living in the Global South and in (ex)colonies. Breadwinner models and the racialisation of citizenship made for exclusions. I don't want to return to the same welfare settlement if returning maintains those exclusions. Nostalgia is really common in discussions of work, for example, alienating factory work replaced more fulfilling craft work; alienating call centre work replaced factory work where at least you had your mates and your union. It always depends on what comparison is being made, on whose behalf.

The person who says 'I think there's a problem with this way of thinking' need not be the person or people who say, 'I know, I can give you a solution.' As an idiot, not a critic, my aim has been to ask new questions. At the start of the book, I talked about the limits of solutionism. I don't think that the answers to the problem of work will be found in a book. Poisons are best dealt with using specific kinds of cures; universal remedies aren't that effective. How different poisons feed on each other and depend on each other and the way something is a poison in one situation but neutral or beneficial in another complicates the questions of cures. 'Guardians' offer logical solutions and technological fixes. In the context of environmental crisis, geoengineering has started to promise that it has radical solutions – but with a radical uncertainty about its effectiveness. That might not cause hesitation because of the potential profit making that emerges: state-sponsored investment to benefit private sector firms. The fictional promise may soon 'try to impose itself, as the only "logical" solution, whether we like it or not'.[17]

There are, however, always and already many ways in which 'common-sense' accounts that privilege the economic are on the defensive, and current norms and systems are under question. And even some taken for granted elements of contemporary life produced by neoliberal, technocratic systems are biting back. Structures and systems are being nibbled at, infested by diseases of their own making. They are being destabilised. The resurgence of worker activism is one such bite back; another is that nature has exceeded its position as a *resource* for human flourishing and refuses to be ignored. Computation (IT), on which governance relies and which gathers and assesses data about populations, communities and atomised consumers, is under question for the unholy powers it has claimed. And it is good to remember the essential con of cyber-capitalism: the claim, assumption and certainty that IT works, and that if it doesn't work, the user is at fault. And even though many have talked about the progressive invasion of markets into private spaces, the domestic, the informal and the everyday of care and repair are also spaces for bite-back. Here the limits of market reasoning and the complexity of 'work' become very visible. There are already diverse economies, where the ethics of work is also an ethics of life itself.

Notes

Chapter One: Framing the present: capitalism, work and crisis

[1] Stengers (2005).
[2] Glucksmann (1995); Mies (1986); Weeks (2011).
[3] Stengers (2015).
[4] Danowski and Viveiros de Castro (2017, p 15).
[5] Ingold (2017, p XX).
[6] Fuller and Goffey (2013).
[7] Kidder et al (2014).
[8] ILO (2018).
[9] Stengers (2015, p 9).
[10] Nelson (2004).
[11] Streeck (2016).
[12] Hirschman (1992).
[13] Fligstein (2001).
[14] Gibson–Graham (1996, 2006).
[15] Gibson–Graham (1996, p 2).
[16] Gibson Graham (2006, p xxi).
[17] Gibson–Graham (1996, p 41).
[18] Gibson–Graham (1996, p 142).
[19] Gibson–Graham (2006, p xxv).
[20] Roelvink et al (2015).
[21] Chakrabarty (2009).
[22] Widdows and Smith (2011).
[23] Bolton (2007, p 7).
[24] Benhabib (1986, p 411).
[25] Puig de la Bellacasa (2017).
[26] Nixon (2011).
[27] Stengers and Ralet (1997, p 222).
[28] Fassin (2012, 2013).
[29] Henriksson (2015).
[30] Streeck (2016).
[31] Morozov (2013).

Chapter Two: Production is work, is work production?

[1] Illouz (2007).
[2] Boltanski and Chiapello (2005).
[3] Goldthorpe et al (1969).
[4] Marcuse (1964).
[5] Blauner (1964).
[6] Braverman (1974).
[7] For example, Burawoy (1979).
[8] Boltanski and Chiapello (2005).
[9] Grote and Guest (2017).
[10] Strangleman (2005).
[11] Strathern (2006, p 196).
[12] Amoore (2000).
[13] Roy (1959).
[14] Roy (1959, p 291).
[15] Roy (1959, p 299).
[16] Chira and Einhorn (2017).
[17] Omi and Winant (2014).
[18] Glenn (2002).
[19] Pierce (2012).
[20] Chakrabarty (2008, p 7).
[21] Bhambra (2007, p 137).
[22] Chandavarkar (1994).
[23] Liu (2010).
[24] Wallerstein (2004).
[25] Williams (1944 [1994]).
[26] Pulido (2017).
[27] Crosby (1986).
[28] McGuire and Laaser (2018).
[29] Bales (2016).
[30] Boutang (2012).
[31] Pavlovskaya (2015).
[32] Larner (2003).
[33] Amoore (2002).
[34] Peck and Theodore (2007).
[35] Mohanty (2003).
[36] Esteva and Prakash (1998).
[37] Tsing (2009).
[38] Tokatli (2003).
[39] Barrientos (2013).
[40] Barrientos et al (2011).
[41] Gold et al (2015).
[42] Phillips and Mieres (2015).
[43] Ross (2008).
[44] Urry (2014).
[45] Cowen (2014, p 58).

[46] Barrientos (2013).

[47] Mah (2014).

[48] Chua (2015).

Chapter Three: Deleted labour and hidden work

[1] Frase (2016); Rifkin (1995). Note how long Rifkin's prophecy is taking to come true.

[2] Trentmann (2007).

[3] Cobble (1991).

[4] Kabeer (2004).

[5] Tsing (2015).

[6] Scott (2012).

[7] Davies (2015).

[8] Santos (2004, p 166).

[9] Gibson–Graham (2008).

[10] Glucksmann (1995); Taylor (2004).

[11] Hatton (2017, p 337).

[12] Star (1991, pp 278-9).

[13] Lorde (2017).

[14] Gibson–Graham (1996, p 12).

[15] Pahl (1984).

[16] Moya (2007).

[17] Sen (2009, p 324).

[18] Glucksmann (1995, 2005).

[19] Puig de la Bellacasa (2017).

[20] Strasser (1982).

[21] Cowan (1983).

[22] Altintas and Sullivan (2016).

[23] McDowell et al (2009).

[24] Glucksmann (2014).

[25] De Stefano (2015).

[26] Pahl (1984).

[27] Pettinger et al (2005).

[28] Krinsky and Simonet (2017).

[29] Adams (2012).

[30] Grimshaw et al (2002, p 489).

[31] Agar (2003).

Chapter Four: How does a body work?

[1] Bolton (2007).

[2] Hodson (2001).

[3] McCabe (2009).

[4] Hesmondhalgh and Baker (2010).

[5] Bolton (2007).

[6] Kabeer (2000).

[7] Edwards (2003, p 185).

8   Simone (2015, pp 375-6).
9   Bowker and Star (1999, p 39).
10 Orr (1996).
11 Lee (2018).
12 Pettinger (2015).
13 Ingold (2011, p 211).
14 Sennett (2008).
15 Lande (2007).
16 Lyon and Back (2012).
17 Berner (2008).
18 Ong (1987).
19 Wolkowitz (2006).
20 Whyte (1946, p 123).
21 Hochschild (2003).
22 Illouz (2007).
23 Büscher (2007).

Chapter Five: Work now

1   Mirowski and Plehwe (2009).
2   Venugopal (2015).
3   Peck (2008).
4   Harvey (2005).
5   Dean (2014).
6   Brenner et al (2010).
7   Vail (2018).
8   Brenner et al (2010, p 203).
9   Fourcade (2006).
10 Larner (2003, p 510).
11 The cover uses an extract from Rivera's 'Making of a Fresco', a painting about making a mural of a worker.
12 Capaldo and Izurieta (2013, p 1).
13 Vail (2018).
14 Larner (2003).
15 Luckman et al (2009).
16 Ong (2006).
17 Orta (2013).
18 Timmermans and Epstein (2010).
19 Amoore (2000).
20 Dardot and Laval (2014, p 255).
21 Larner (2003).
22 Harris and Scully (2015, p 416).
23 Siegmann and Schiphorst (2016, p 112).
24 Rabinbach (1990).
25 Gregg (2011).
26 Schultz (2015).
27 Hatton (2011).

28 Fu (2016).
29 Fu (2016).
30 Fu (2016, p 1).
31 Fu (2016).
32 Gutelius (2015).
33 Freeman (2000).
34 Baines et al (2017).
35 Hardt and Negri (2009, p 146).
36 Herod and Lambert (2016)
37 Campbell and Price (2016).
38 Campbell and Price (2016, p 318).
39 Lee and Kofman (2012, p 389).
40 Kalleberg (2011).
41 Herod and Lambert (2016, p 17)
42 Lee and Kofman (2012).
43 Lee and Kofman (2012, pp 394-6).
44 Harris and Scully (2015).

End of Part One: Everyday life, technology and environment in the present

1 Dalakoglou (2010).
2 Barbrook and Cameron (1996).
3 Lovink (2009, p 88).
4 Bakker (2010).

Chapter Six: Informal work and everyday life

1   Bhowmik (2010).
2   Williams (2006).
3   Ledeneva (1998).
4   ILO (2018).
5   Santos (2004).
6   Portes et al (1989).
7   Bieler et al (2008).
8   Harris and Scully (2015).
9   Ferreira (2016).
10 Mizen and Ofuso-Kusi (2013).
11 Benería (2008).
12 Charmes (2016).
13 Charmes (2016).
14 Simone (2004); Simone and Fauzan (2013).
15 Botoeva (2014).
16 Williams (2004).
17 Williams (2004).
18 Williams (2004, p 11).
19 Urry (2014).
20 Anderson (2010).

21 Pajnik (2016).
22 Pajnik (2016).
23 Garvey and Bareto (2016).
24 Gregg (2011).
25 Mies (1986).
26 Lee and Kofman (2012).
27 Joynt and Webster (2016).
28 Momsen (2003).
29 Momsen (2003, p 1).
30 Parreñas (2015).
31 Chin (1998).
32 Zelizer (2005).
33 Sharma (2014).
34 Abílio (2012).
35 Hattatoğlu and Tate (2016).

Chapter Seven: Technology

1   Grint and Woolgar (1997); Wajcman (2006).
2   Cockburn (1983, p 12).
3   Kraft (1979).
4   Kraft (1979, p 143).
5   Ensmenger (2012).
6   Wajcman (2006).
7   Rood (2017, p 2).
8   Banerjee (1995).
9   Mirchandani (2012).
10 Aneesh (2006).
11 Cited in Brophy (2006).
12 Shestakofksy (2017).
13 Mas et al (2017, p 18, figure 13).
14 Mas et al (2017, p 19, figure 14).
15 Apri (2007, p 15). Figures derived from ISIC categories, the UN system for classifying economic activity by industrial sector.
16 OECD (2014, p 18, figure 8).
17 OECD (2016, p 6).
18 Varying from almost 6 per cent in Finland to under 2 per cent in Greece, Lithuania and Romania (EU Labour Force Survey, cited in OECD, 2014, p 15).
19 OECD (2014, p 12).
20 Moore (2017).
21 Scheiber (2017).
22 Berkeley (1949).
23 Autor (2014).
24 Heilbroner (1965, pp 34-6), cited in Autor (2014, p 4).
25 Bowker and Star (1999).
26 Knox et al (2007).

27 Knox et al (2007, p 30).
28 Fuller and Goffey (2012).
29 Shestakofksy (2017).
30 Ó Riain (2010).
31 Kennedy (2016).
32 Burak (2017).
33 Strauss et al (1985, p 189).
34 Fox et al (1998).
35 Sullivan and Wyatt (2006).
36 Nielsen (2017).
37 Barley (1986).
38 Barrett et al (2012).
39 Fotaki and Hyde (2015).
40 Miller et al (2008).
41 Goffey et al (2014).
42 Bloomfield (1995); Bloomfield and Danieli (1995).

Chapter Eight: Green work

1   Roelvink (2015).
2   Gregson et al (2014).
3   Moore and Robbins (2015).
4   Nixon (2011).
5   Kidder et al (2014).
6   Freidberg (2009).
7   Singh (2013).
8   Cumbers et al (2017).
9   Renner et al (2008, p 34).
10 Hess (2012, p 63).
11 Crowley (1999, p 1017).
12 Renner et al (2008, p 7).
13 Renner et al (2008, p 13).
14 Stevis (2013).
15 Masterman–Smith (2010).
16 Obach (2004).
17 Snell and Fairbrother (2013).
18 Goods (2014).
19 Hess (2012).
20 Hess (2012, p 48).
21 Hess (2012, p 214).
22 Renner et al (2008).
23 Graham and Thrift (2007, p 13).
24 Graham and Thrift (2007).
25 Pellow and Park (2002).
26 Wheeler and Glucksmann (2015).
27 Obeng-Odoom (2014).
28 Milgram (2010).

29 Bozkurt and Stowell (2016).
30 Crang et al (2012).
31 Gregson et al (2014).
32 Pajnik (2016).
33 Pajnik (2016).
34 Dauvergne and LeBaron (2013).
35 Dauvergne and LeBaron (2013).
36 Nightingale (2005).
37 Goldman (2001).
38 Goldman (2001, p 202).
39 Craig et al (1993).
40 Holling and Meffe (1996).
41 Holling and Meffe (1996, p 334).
42 Hess (2012).
43 MacGregor (2009).
44 Ross (1996, p 10).
45 Buck et al (2013).
46 Stengers (2015, p 9).
47 Bingham (2008).
48 Goffey and Pettinger (2014).
49 Fassin (2012, 2013).
50 Dauvergne and LeBaron (2013).

Chapter Nine: Biting back

1 Silver (2003).
2 Danyluk (2018).
3 ILO (1999, p 3).
4 Miller (2004).
5 Fichter and Stevis (2013).
6 Mathews (2018).
7 Hugill et al (2016).
8 Lim and Prakash (2017).
9 McCann and Fudge (2017).
10 Burchell et al (2014); Green (2006).
11 Kalleberg (2011).
12 Puig de la Bellacasa (2017).
13 Timms (2012).
14 Streeck (2016).
15 Chun (2016).
16 Figart (2017).
17 Stengers (2015, pp 8-9).

References

Abílio, L.C. (2012) 'Making up exploitation: Direct selling, cosmetics and forms of precarious labour in modern Brazil', *International Journal of Management Concepts and Philosophy* 6(1), 59-70.

Adams, V. (2012) 'The other road to serfdom: Recovery by the market and the affect economy in New Orleans', *Public Culture* 24(1[66]), 185-216 (https://doi.org/10.1215/08992363-1443601).

Agar, J. (2003) *The government machine: A revolutionary history of the computer*, Cambridge, MA: MIT Press.

Altintas, E. and Sullivan, O. (2016) 'Fifty years of change updated: Cross-national gender convergence in housework', *Demographic Research* 35, 455-70.

Amoore, L. (2000) 'International political economy and the "contested firm"', *New Political Economy* 5(2), 183-204.

Amoore, L. (2002) *Globalization contested: An international political economy of work*, Manchester: Manchester University Press.

Anderson, B. (2010) 'Migration, immigration controls and the fashioning of precarious workers', *Work, Employment and Society* 24(2), 300-17 (https://doi.org/10.1177/0950017010362141).

Aneesh, A. (2006) *Virtual migration: The programming of globalization*, Durham, NC: Duke University Press.

Apri, D. (2007) *Working Party on indicators for the information society: Classifying information and communication technology (ICT) Services*, Paris: OECD Publishing.

Autor, D. (2014) *Polanyi's paradox and the shape of employment growth*, Working Paper No 20485, Cambridge, MA: National Bureau of Economic Research, Inc.

Baines, D., Cunningham, I. and Shields, J. (2017) 'Filling the gaps: Unpaid (and precarious) work in the nonprofit social services', *Critical Social Policy* 37(4), 625-45.

Bakker, K. (2010) 'The limits of "neoliberal natures": Debating green neoliberalism', *Progress in Human Geography* 34(6), 715-35 (https://doi.org/10.1177/0309132510376849).

Bales, K. (2016) *Blood and earth: Modern slavery, ecocide, and the secret to saving the world*, New York: Random House.

Banerjee, N. (1995) 'Something old, something new, something borrowed... The electronics industry in Calcutta', in S. Mitter and S. Rowbotham (eds) *Women encounter technology: Changing patterns of employment in the third world*, 1, 233, London and New York: Routledge.

Barbrook, R. and Cameron, A. (1996) 'The Californian ideology', *Science as Culture* 6(1), 44-72.

Barley, S.R. (1986) 'Technology as an occasion for structuring: Evidence from observations of CT scanners and the social order of radiology departments', *Administrative Science Quarterly* 78-108.

Barnett, C. (2005) 'The consolation of "neoliberalism"', *Geoforum* 36(1), 7-12.

Barrett, M., Oborn, E., Orlikowski, W.J. and Yates, J. (2012) 'Reconfiguring boundary relations: Robotic innovations in pharmacy work', *Organization Science* 23(5), 1448-66 (https://doi.org/10.1287/orsc.1100.0639).

Barrientos, S.W. (2013) '"Labour chains": Analysing the role of labour contractors in global production networks', *Journal of Development Studies* 49(8), 1058-71 (https://doi.org/10.1080/00220388.2013.780040).

Barrientos, S., Gereffi, G. and Rossi, A. (2011) 'Economic and social upgrading in global production networks: A new paradigm for a changing world', *International Labour Review* 150(3-4), 319-40.

Benería, L. (2008) 'The crisis of care, international migration, and public policy', *Feminist Economics* 14(3), 1-21. doi:10.1080/13545700802081984

Benhabib, S. (1986) 'The generalized and the concrete other: The Kohlberg–Gilligan controversy and feminist theory in feminism as critique', *Praxis International* 5(4), 402-24.

Berkeley, E.C. (1949) *Giant brains: Or, Machines that think*, New York: Wiley.

Berner, B. (2008) 'Working knowledge as performance: On the practical understanding of machines', *Work, Employment and Society* 22(2), 319-36.

Bhambra, G.K. (2007) *Rethinking modernity: Post-colonialism and the sociological imagination*, Basingstoke: Palgrave.

Bhowmik, S. (ed) (2010) *Street vendors in the global urban economy*, New Delhi: Routledge, Taylor and Francis.

Bieler, A., Lindberg, I. and Pillay, D. (2008) *Labour and challenges of globalisation: What prospects for transnational solidarity?*, London and Ann Arbor, MI: Pluto Press.

Bingham, N. (2008) 'Slowing things down: Lessons from the GM controversy', *Geoforum* 39(1), 111-22.

Blauner, R. (1964) *Alienation and freedom: The factory worker and his industry*, Oxford: Chicago University Press.

Boltanski, L. and Chiapello, E. (2005) *The new spirit of capitalism*, London: Verso.

Bolton, S.C. (2007) *Dignity in and at work: Why it matters, Dimensions of dignity at work*, Oxford: Butterworth-Heinemann.

Botoeva, G. (2014) 'Hashish as cash in a post-Soviet Kyrgyz village', *International Journal of Drug Policy* 25(6), 1227-34.

Boutang, Y.M. (2012) *Cognitive capitalism*, Cambridge: Polity.

Bowker, G. and Star, S.L. (1999) *Sorting things out: Classification and its consequences*, Cambridge, MA: MIT Press.

Bowker, G.C., Timmermans, S., Clarke, A.E. and Balka, E. (eds) (2015) *Boundary objects and beyond: Working with Leigh Star*, Cambridge, MA: MIT Press.

Bozkurt, Ö. and Stowell, A. (2016) 'Skills in the green economy: Recycling promises in the UK e-waste management sector', *New Technology, Work and Employment* 31(2), 146-60.

Braverman, H. (1974) *Labor and monopoly capital*, New York: Monthly Review Press.

Brenner, N., Peck, J. and Theodore, N. (2010) 'Variegated neoliberalization: Geographies, modalities, pathways', *Global Networks* 10(2), 182-222.

Brophy, E. (2006) 'System error: Labour precarity and collective organizing at Microsoft', *Canadian Journal of Communication* 31(3), October.

Buck, H.J., Gammon, A.R. and Preston, C.J. (2013) 'Gender and geoengineering', *Hypatia* 29(3), 651-69.

Burak, C. (2017) 'German banker takes 6 months to count 1.2 million inheritance pennies by hand', 16 December (www.dw.com/en/german-banker-takes-6-months-to-count-12-million-inheritance-pennies-by-hand/a-41820835).

Burawoy, M. (1979) *Manufacturing consent: Changes in the labor process under monopoly capitalism*, Chicago, IL: University of Chicago Press.

Burchell, B., Sehnbruch, K., Piasna, A. and Agloni, N. (2014) 'The quality of employment and decent work: Definitions, methodologies, and ongoing debates', *Cambridge Journal of Economics* 38(2), 459-77.

Büscher, M. (2007) 'Interaction in motion: Embodied conduct in emergency teamwork', In *Proceedings of the 2nd Congress of the International Society for Gesture Studies*, ISGS 16.

Campbell, I. and Price, R. (2016) 'Precarious work and precarious workers: Towards an improved conceptualisation', *The Economic and Labour Relations Review* 27(3), 314-32.

Capaldo, J. and Izurieta, A. (2013) 'The imprudence of labour market flexibilization in a fiscally austere world', *International Labour Review* 52(1), 1-26.

Castree, N. (2006) 'From neoliberalism to neoliberalisation: Consolations, confusions, and necessary illusions', *Environment and Planning A: International Journal of Urban and Regional Research* 38(1), 1-6.

Chakrabarty, D. (2008) *Provincializing Europe: Postcolonial thought and historical difference*, Reissue, Princeton, NJ: Princeton University Press.

Chakrabarty, D. (2009) 'The climate of history: Four theses', *Critical Inquiry* 35(2), 197-222.

Chandavarkar, R. (1994) *The origins of industrial capitalism in India: Business strategies and the working classes in Bombay, 1900-40*, Cambridge: Cambridge University Press.

Charmes, J. (2016) 'The informal economy: Definitions, size, contribution and main characteristics', in E. Kraemer-Mbula and S. Wunsch-Vincent (eds) *The informal economy in developing nations*, Cambridge: Cambridge University Press, pp 13-52 (https://doi.org/10.1017/CBO9781316662076.006).

Chira, S. and Einhorn, C. (2017) 'How tough is it to change a culture of harassment? Ask women at Ford', *New York Times*, 19 December (www.nytimes.com/interactive/2017/12/19/us/ford-chicago-sexual-harassment.html).

Chin, C.B. (1998) *In service and servitude: Foreign female domestic workers and the Malaysian 'Modernity' project*, New York: Columbia University Press.

Chua, C. (2015) 'Slow boat to China', Blog series (https://thedisorderofthings.com/tag/slow-boat-to-china/).

Chun, J.J. (2016) 'Organizing across divides: Union challenges to precarious work in Vancouver's privatized health care sector', *Progress in Development Studies* 16(2), 173-88 (https://doi.org/10.1177/1464993415623132).

Cobble, D.S. (1991) 'Organizing the postindustrial workforce: Lessons from the history of waitress unionism', *Industrial and Labor Relations Review* 44(3), 419-36.

Cockburn, C. (1983) *Brothers: Male dominance and technological change*, London: Pluto.

Cowan, R.S. (1983) *More work for mother: The ironies of household technology from the open hearth to the microwave*, New York: Chatto & Windus.

Cowen, D. (2014) *The deadly life of logistics: Mapping violence in global trade*, Minneapolis, MN: University of Minnesota Press.

Craig, P.P., Glasser, H. and Kempton, W. (1993) 'Ethics and values in environmental policy: The said and the UNCED', *Environmental Values* 2(2), 137-57.

Crang, M., Gregson, N., Ahamed, F., Ferdous, R. and Akhter, N. (2012) 'Death, the phoenix and Pandora: Transforming things and values in Bangladesh', in C. Alexander and J. Reno (eds) *Economies of recycling: The global transformation of materials, values and social relations*. London and New York: Zed Books, pp 59-75.

Crosby, A. (1986) *Ecological imperialism*, Cambridge: Cambridge University Press.

Crowley, K. (1999) 'Jobs and environment: The "double dividend" of ecological modernisation?', *International Journal of Social Economics* 26(7/8/9), 1013-27.

Cumbers, A., Shaw, D., Crossan, J. and McMaster, R. (2017) 'The work of community gardens: Reclaiming place for community in the city', *Work, Employment and Society*, 0950017017695042.

Dalakoglou, D. (2010) 'The road: An ethnography of the Albanian–Greek cross-border motorway', *American Ethnologist* 37(1), 132-49.

Danowski, D. and Viveiros de Castro, E. (2017) *The ends of the world*, Malden, MA: Polity Press.

Danyluk, M. (2018) 'Capital's logistical fix: Accumulation, globalization, and the survival of capitalism', *Environment and Planning D: Society and Space* 36(4), 630-47 (https://doi.org/10.1177/0263775817703663).

Dardot, P. and Laval, C. (2014) *The new way of the world: On neoliberal society*, London: Verso Books.

Dauvergne, P. and LeBaron, G. (2013) 'The social cost of environmental solutions', *New Political Economy* 18(3), 410-30 (https://doi.org/10.1080/13563467.2012.740818).

Davies, T. (2015) 'Nuclear borders: Informally negotiating the Chernobyl Exclusion Zone', in J. Morris and A. Polese (eds) *Informal economies in post-socialist spaces: Practices, institutions and networks*, London: Palgrave Macmillan, pp 225-44.

De Stefano, V. (2015) 'The rise of the "just-in-time workforce": On-demand work, crowd work and labour protection in the "gig-economy"', *SSRN Electronic Journal* (https://doi.org/10.2139/ssrn.2682602).

Dean, M. (2014) 'Rethinking neoliberalism', *Journal of Sociology* 50(2), 150-63.

Edwards, P.N. (2003) 'Infrastructure and modernity: Force, time, and social organization in the history of sociotechnical systems', in P. Brey, A. Feenberg and T. Misa (eds) *Modernity and technology*, Cambridge, MA: MIT Press, pp 185-225.

Ensmenger, N.L. (2012) *The computer boys take over: Computers, programmers, and the politics of technical expertise*, Cambridge, MA and London: MIT Press.

Esteva, G. and Prakash, M.S. (1998) *Grassroots post-modernism: Re-making the soil of cultures*, London: Zed.

Fassin, D. (2012) *Humanitarian reason: A moral history of the present*, Berkeley, CA: University of California Press.

Fassin, D. (2013) *Enforcing order: An ethnography of urban policing*, New York: Polity.

Fassin, D. (2015) *Four lectures on ethics: Anthropological perspectives* (with Veena Das, Michael Lambek and Webb Keane), Chicago, IL: Hau Books.

Ferreira, M. (2016) 'Informal versus precarious work in Colombia: Concept and operationalization', *Progress in Development Studies* 16(2), 140–58 (https://doi.org/10.1177/1464993415623128).

Fichter, M. and Stevis, D. (2013) *Global framework agreements in a union-hostile environment: The case of the USA*, Berlin: Friedrich Ebert Stiftung.

Figart, D.M. (2017) *Stories of progressive institutional change*, Basingstoke: Palgrave Macmillan.

Fligstein, N. (2001) *The architecture of markets: An economic sociology of 21st century capitalist societies*, Princeton, NJ: Princeton University Press.

Fotaki, M. and Hyde, P. (2015) 'Organizational blind spots: Splitting, blame and idealization in the National Health Service', *Human Relations* 68, 441–62.

Fourcade, M. (2006) 'The construction of a global profession: The transnationalization of economics', *American Journal of Sociology* 112(1), 145–94 (https://doi.org/10.1086/502693).

Fox, J., Johns, N. and Rahmanzadeh, A. (1998) 'Disseminating medical knowledge: The PROforma approach', *Artificial Intelligence in Medicine* 14(1), 157–82.

Frase, P. (2016) *Four futures: Life after capitalism*, London: Verso.

Freeman, C. (2000) *High tech and high heels in the global economy: Women, work, and pink-collar identities in the Caribbean*, Durham, NC: Duke University Press.

Freidberg, S. (2009) *Fresh: A perishable history*, Cambridge, MA: Harvard University Press.

Fu, H. (2016) *Temporary agency work and globalisation: Beyond flexibility and inequality*, London: Routledge.

Fuller, M. and Goffey, A. (2012) *Evil media*, Cambridge, MA and London: MIT Press.

Fuller, M. and Goffey, A. (2013) 'The unknown objects of object-orientation', in P. Harvey, E. Casella, G. Evans, H. Knox, C. Mclean, E. Silva et al (eds) *Objects and materials: A Routledge companion*, London: Routledge, pp 218–26.

Gabrys, J. (2011) *Digital rubbish: A natural history of electronics*, Ann Arbor, MI: University of Michigan Press.

Garvey, B. and Barreto, M.J. (2016) 'At the cutting edge: Precarious work in Brazil's sugar and ethanol industry', in R. Lambert and A. Herod (eds) *Neoliberal capitalism and precarious work: Ethnographies of accommodation and resistance*, Cheltenham and Northampton, MA: Edward Elgar, pp 166-204.

Gibson-Graham, J.K. (1996) *The end of capitalism (as we knew it): A feminist critique of political economy*, Oxford: Blackwell.

Gibson-Graham, J.K. (2006) *A postcapitalist politics*, Minneapolis, MN: University of Minnesota Press.

Gibson-Graham, J.K. (2008) 'Diverse economies: Performative practices for "other worlds"', *Progress in Human Geography* 32(5), 613-32 (https://doi.org/10.1177/0309132508090821).

Glenn, E.N. (2002) *Unequal freedom: How race and gender shaped American citizenship and labor*, Cambridge, MA: Harvard University Press.

Glucksmann, M.A. (1995) 'Why "work"? Gender and the "total social organization of labour"', *Gender, Work and Organization* 2(2), 63-75.

Glucksmann, M.A. (2005) 'Shifting boundaries and interconnections: Extending the "total social organisation of labour"', *The Sociological Review* 53(2 [Suppl]), 19-36 (https://journals.sagepub.com/doi/10.1111/j.1467-954X.2005.00570.x).

Glucksmann, M.A. (2014) 'Bake or buy? Comparative and theoretical perspectives on divisions of labour in food preparation work', *Anthropology of Food* [Online], S10 (http://aof.revues.org/7691).

Goffey, A. and Pettinger, L. (2014) 'Refrains and assemblages: Exploring market negotiations and green subjectivity with Guattari', *Subjectivity* 7(4), 385-410.

Goffey, A., Pettinger, L. and Speed, E. (2014) 'Politics, policy and privatisation in the everyday experience of big data in the NHS', in M. Hand and S. Hillyard (eds) *Studies in qualitative methodology* (Vol 13), Emerald Group Publishing Limited, pp 31-50.

Gold, S., Trautrims, A. and Trodd, Z. (2015) 'Modern slavery challenges to supply chain management', *Supply Chain Management: An International Journal* 20(5), 485-94 (https://doi.org/10.1108/SCM-02-2015-0046).

Goldman, M. (2001) 'The birth of a discipline: Producing authoritative green knowledge, World Bank-style', *Ethnography* 2(2), 191-217.

Goldthorpe, J., Lockwood D., Bechhofer, F. and Platt, J. (1969) *The affluent worker in the class structure*, Cambridge: Cambridge University Press.

Goods, C. (2014) *Greening auto jobs: A critical analysis of the green job solution*, Lanham, MD: Lexington Books.

Graham, M., Hjorth, I. and Lehdonvirta, V. (2017) 'Digital labour and development: Impacts of global digital labour platforms and the gig economy on worker livelihoods', *Transfer: European Review of Labour and Research* 23(2), 135-62.

Graham, S. and Thrift, N. (2007) 'Out of order: Understanding repair and maintenance', *Theory, Culture and Society* 24(3), 1-25.

Green, F. (2006) *Demanding work: The paradox of job quality in the affluent economy*, Woodstock: Princeton University Press.

Gregg, M. (2011) *Work's intimacy*, Cambridge: Polity Press.

Gregson, N., Crang, M., Botticello, J., Calestani, M. and Krzywoszynska, A. (2014) 'Doing the "dirty work" of the green economy: Resource recovery and migrant labour in the EU', *European Urban and Regional Studies* 23(4), 1-15.

Grimshaw, D., Vincent, S. and Willmott, H. (2002) 'Going privately: Partnership and outsourcing in UK public services', *Public Administration* 80(3), 475-502.

Grint, K. and Woolgar, S. (1997) *The machine at work: Technology, work and organization*, Cambridge: Polity Press.

Grote, G. and Guest, D. (2017) 'The case for reinvigorating quality of working life research', *Human Relations* 70(2), 149-67.

Gutelius, B. (2015) 'Disarticulating distribution: Labor segmentation and subcontracting in global logistics', *Geoforum* 60, 53-61.

Hallin, A., Crevani, L., Ivory, C. and Mörndal, M. (2017) 'Digitalisation and work: Sociomaterial entanglements in steel production', *Nordisk företagsekonomisk förening (NFF)*, Bodø, Norway.

Hardt, M. and Negri, A. (2009) *Commonwealth*, Cambridge, MA: Harvard University Press.

Harris, K. and Scully, B. (2015) 'A hidden counter-movement? Precarity, politics, and social protection before and beyond the neoliberal era', *Theory and Society* 44(5), 415-44 (https://doi.org/10.1007/s11186-015-9256-5).

Harvey, D. (2005) *A brief history of neoliberalism*, Oxford: Oxford University Press.

Hattatoğlu, D. and Tate, J. (2016) 'Home-based work and new ways of organizing in the era of globalization', in R. Lambert and A. Herod (eds) *Neoliberal capitalism and precarious work: Ethnographies of accommodation and resistance*, Cheltenham: Edward Elgar, pp 96-124.

Hatton, E. (2011) *The temp economy: From Kelly Girls to Permatemps in postwar America*, Philadelphia, PA: Temple University Press.

Hatton, E. (2017) 'Mechanisms of invisibility: Rethinking the concept of invisible work', *Work, Employment and Society* 31(2), 336-51.

Henriksson, L. (2015) 'Can autoworkers save the climate?', *Jacobin*, 10 February (www.jacobinmag.com/2015/10/cars-jobs-climate-change-auto-industry-ford-gm-lucas-aerospace-alternative-production/).

Herod, A. and Lambert, R. (2016) 'Neoliberalism, precarious work and remaking the geography of global capitalism', in R. Lambert and A. Herod (eds) *Neoliberal capitalism and precarious work: Ethnographies of accommodation and resistance*, Cheltenham: Edward Elgar Publishing, pp 1-42.

Hesmondhalgh, D. and Baker, S. (2010) *Creative labour: Media work in three cultural industries*, London and New York: Routledge.

Hess, D. (2012) *Good green jobs in a global economy: Making and keeping new industries in the United States*, Cambridge, MA: MIT Press.

Hirschman, A.O. (1992) *Rival views of market society and other recent essays*, New York: Viking Penguin.

Hochschild, A.R. (2003) *The managed heart: Commercialization of human feeling*, Berkeley, CA: University of California Press

Hodson, R. (2001) *Dignity at work*, Cambridge: Cambridge University Press.

Holling, C.S. and Meffe, G.K. (1996) 'Command and control and the pathology of natural resource management', *Conservation Biology* 10(2), 328-37.

Hugill, A.R., Short, J.L. and Toffel, M.W. (2016) *Beyond symbolic responses to private politics: Examining labor standards improvement in global supply chains*, Harvard Business School Working Paper, No 17-001.

Illouz, E. (2007) *Cold intimacies: The making of emotional capitalism*, Cambridge: Polity Press.

ILO (International Labour Organization) (1999) *Decent work*, Report of the Director-General, International Labour Conference, 87th Session, Geneva: ILO.

ILO (2017) *Global estimates of modern slavery: Forced labour and forced marriage*, Geneva: ILO.

ILO (2018) *Women and men in the informal economy: A statistical picture* (3rd edn), Geneva: ILO.

Ingold, T. (2011) *Being alive: Essays on movement, knowledge and description*, London: Routledge.

Ingold, T. (2017) 'On human correspondence', *Journal of the Royal Anthropological Institute* 23, 9-27.

Joynt, K. and Webster, E. (2016) 'The growth and organisation of a precariat: Working in the clothing industry in Johannesburg's inner city', in R. Lambert, and A. Herod (eds) *Globalization and precarious work: Ethnographies of accommodation and resistance*, Cheltenham and Northampton, MA: Edward Elgar.

Kabeer, N. (2000) *The power to choose: Bangladeshi women and labour market decisions in London and Dhaka*, London: Verso Books.

Kabeer, N. (2004) 'Globalization, labor standards, and women's rights: Dilemmas of collective (in) action in an interdependent world', *Feminist Economics* 10(1), 3-35.

Kalleberg, A. (2011) *Good jobs, bad jobs: The rise of polarized and precarious employment systems in the United States, 1970s to 2000s*, New York: Russell Sage.

Kennedy, H. (2016) *Post, mine, repeat: Social media data mining becomes ordinary*, Basingstoke: Palgrave Macmillan UK.

Kidder, T., Mapandi, Z. and Ortega, H. (2014) 'Not "women's burden": How washing clothes and grinding corn became issues of social justice and development', *Gender and Development* 22(3), 495-513.

Knox, H., O'Doherty, D., Vurdubakis, T. and Westrup, C. (2007) 'Transformative capacity, information technology, and the making of business "experts"', *The Sociological Review* 55(1), 22-41.

Kraft, P. (1979) 'The routinizing of computer programming', *Sociology of Work and Occupations* 6(2), 139-55.

Krinsky, J. and Simonet, M. (2017) *Who cleans your park? Public work and urban governance in New York City*, Chicago, IL: University of Chicago Press.

Lambert, R. and Herod, A. (2016) (eds) *Neoliberal capitalism and precarious work: Ethnographies of accommodation and resistance*, Cheltenham and Northampton, MA: Edward Elgar.

Lande, B. (2007) 'Breathing like a soldier: Culture incarnate', *The Sociological Review* 55(s1), 95-108.

Larner, W. (2003) 'Neoliberalism?', *Environment and Planning D: Society and Space* 21(5), 509-12.

Ledeneva, A.V. (1998) *Russia's economy of favours: Blat, networking and informal exchange*, Cambridge: Cambridge University Press.

Lee, C.K. and Kofman, Y. (2012) 'The politics of precarity: Views beyond the United States', *Work and Occupations* 39(4), 388-408.

Lee, T.B. (2018) 'Production hell', *Ars Technica*, 22 April (https://arstechnica.com/cars/2018/04/experts-say-tesla-has-repeated-car-industry-mistakes-from-the-1980s/).

Lim, S. and Prakash, A. (2017) 'Do economic problems at home undermine worker safety abroad? A panel study, 1980-2009', *World Development* 96, 56-77 (https://doi.org/10.1016/j.worlddev.2017.03.038).

Liu, X. (2010) *The Silk Road in world history*, Oxford and New York: Oxford University Press.

Lorde, A. (2017) 'The master's tools will never dismantle the master's house', in *Your silence will not protect you: Essays and poems*, London: Silver Press.

Lovink, G. (2009) *Dynamics of critical internet culture: An archive of content production (1994-2001)*, Amsterdam: Institute of Network Cultures.

Luckman, S., Gibson, C. and Lea, T. (2009) 'Mosquitoes in the mix: How transferable is creative city thinking?', *Singapore Journal of Tropical Geography* 30(1), 70-85.

Lyon, D. and Back, L. (2012) 'Fishmongers in a global economy: Craft and social relations on a London market', *Sociological Research Online* [Online] 17.

McCabe, D. (2009) 'Enterprise contested: Betwixt and between the discourses of career and enterprise in a UK bank', *Human Relations* 62(10), 1551-79 (https://doi.org/10.1177/0018726709336499).

McCann, D. and Fudge, J. (2017) 'Unacceptable forms of work: A multidimensional model', *International Labour Review* 156(2), 147-84 (https://doi.org/10.1111/ilr.12002xxx).

McDowell, L., Batnitzky, A. and Dyer, S. (2009) 'Precarious work and economic migration: Emerging immigrant divisions of labour in Greater London's service sector', *International Journal of Urban and Regional Research* 33(1), 3-25 (https://doi.org/10.1111/j.1468-2427.2009.00831.x).

McGuire, D. and Laaser, K. (2018) '"You have to pick": Cotton and state-organized forced labour in Uzbekistan', *Economic and Industrial Democracy* 21 [Online first] (https://doi.org/10.1177/0143831X18789786).

MacGregor, S. (2009) 'A stranger silence still: The need for feminist social research on climate change', *The Sociological Review* 57(s2), 124-40.

Mah, A. (2014) *Port cities and global legacies: Urban identity, Waterfront work, and radicalism*, Basingstoke: Palgrave Macmillan.

Marcuse, H. (1964) *One-dimensional man: Studies in the ideology of advanced industrial society*, Boston, MA: Beacon Press.

Mas, M., Fernández de Guevara, J., Robledo, J.C. and López-Cobo, M. (2017) *The 2017 PREDICT key facts report: An analysis of ICT RandD in the EU and beyond*, Brussels: EU EUR 28594 EN, doi:10.2760/397817.

Masterman-Smith, H. (2010) 'Green collaring a capital crisis?', *Labour and Industry: A Journal of the Social and Economic Relations of Work* 20(3), 317-30.

Mathews, B. (2018) 'Leading Bangladashi textile mill regrets going green', *Apparel Insider*, 11 September (https://apparelinsider.com/leading-bangladashi-textile-mill-regrets-going-green/).

Mies, M. (1986) *Patriarchy and accumulation on a world scale: Women in the international division of labour*, London: Zed.

Milgram, B.L. (2010) 'From trash to totes: Recycled production and cooperative economy practice in the Philippines', *Human Organization* 69(1), 75–85.

Miller, D. (2004) 'Negotiating international framework agreements in the global textile, garment and footwear sector', *Global Social Policy: An Interdisciplinary Journal of Public Policy and Social Development* 4(2), 215–39 (https://doi.org/10.1177/1468018104045110).

Miller, P., Kurunmäki, L. and O'Leary, T. (2008) 'Accounting, hybrids and the management of risk', *Accounting, Organizations and Society* 33(7–8), 942–67.

Mirchandani, K. (2012) *Phone clones: Authenticity in the transnational service economy*, Ithaca, NY: Cornell University Press.

Mirowski, P. and Plehwe, D. (eds) (2009) *The road from Mont Pèlerin: The making of the neoliberal thought collective*, Cambridge, MA: Harvard University Press.

Mizen, P. and Ofosu-Kusi, Y. (2010) 'Asking, giving, receiving: Friendship as survival strategy among Accra's street children', *Childhood* 17(4), 441–54.

Mohanty, C.T. (2003) '"Under Western eyes" revisited: Feminist solidarity through anticapitalist struggles', *Signs: Journal of Women in Culture and Society* 28(2), 499–535 (https://doi.org/10.1086/342914).

Momsen, J.H. (2003) 'Maids on the move', in J.H. Momsen (ed) *Gender, migration and domestic service*, London: Routledge, pp 15–34.

Moore, P. (2017) *The quantified self in precarity: Work, technology, and what counts*, London: Routledge.

Moore, S.A. and Robbins, P. (2015) 'Nature's diverse economies', in G. Roelvink, K. St Martin and J.K. Gibson-Graham (eds) *Making other worlds possible: Performing diverse economies*, Minneapolis, MN: University of Minnesota Press, pp 153–72.

Morozov, E. (2013) *To save everything, click here: Technology, solutionism and the urge to solve problems that don't exist*, London: Allen Lane.

Moya, J.C. (2007) 'Domestic service in a global perspective: Gender, migration, and ethnic niches', *Journal of Ethnic and Migration Studies* 33(4), 559-79.

Nelson, J.A. (2004) 'Clocks, creation and clarity: Insights on ethics and economics from a feminist perspective', *Ethical Theory and Moral Practice* 7(4), 381-98.

Nielsen, M.K. (2017) 'Patient@home: An exploration of good care and the development of welfare technology', Paper presented at Digital Healthcare Symposium, University of Nottingham, 20-21 June.

Nightingale, A.J. (2005) '"The experts taught us all we know": Professionalisation and knowledge in Nepalese community forestry', *Antipode* 37(3), 581-604.

Nixon, R. (2011) *Slow violence and the environmentalism of the poor*, Cambridge, MA: Harvard University Press.

Ó Riain, S. (2010) 'The missing customer and the ever-present market: Software developers and the service economy', *Work and Occupations* 37(3), 320-48.

Obach, B. (2004) *Labor and the environmental movement: The quest for common ground*, Cambridge, MA: MIT Press

Obeng-Odoom, F. (2014) 'Green neoliberalism: Recycling and sustainable urban development in Sekondi-Takoradi', *Habitat International* 41, 129-34.

OECD (Organisation for Economic Co-operation and Development) (2014) *Skills and jobs in the internet economy*, OECD Digital Economy Papers, No 242. Paris: OECD Publishing (http://dx.doi.org/10.1787/5jxvbrjm9bns-en).

OECD (2016) *New skills for the digital economy*, OECD Digital Economy Papers, No 258, Paris: OECD Publishing (https://doi.org/10.1787/5jlwnkm2fc9x-en).

Omi, M. and Winant, H. (2014) *Racial formation in the United States* (3rd edn), New York: Routledge.

Ong, A. (1987) *Spirits of resistance and capitalist discipline: Factory women in Malaysia*, Albany, NY: SUNY Press.

Ong, A. (2006) *Neoliberalism as exception: Mutations of citizenship and sovereignty*, Durham, NC: Duke University Press.

Orr, J.E. (1996) *Talking about machines: An ethnography of a modern job*, Ithaca, NY: Cornell University Press.

Orta, A. (2013) 'Managing the margins: MBA training, international business, and "the value chain of culture"', *American Ethnologist* 40(4), 689-703.

Pahl, R.E. (1984) *Divisions of labour*, Oxford: Blackwell.

Pajnik, M. (2016) '"Wasted precariat": Migrant work in European societies', *Progress in Development Studies* 16(2), 159-72 (https://doi.org/10.1177/1464993415623130).

Parreñas, R. (2015) *Servants of globalization: Migration and domestic work*, Standford, CA: Stanford University Press.

Pavlovskaya, M. (2015) 'Post-soviet welfare and multiple economies of households in Moscow', in K. St Martin, G. Roelvink and J.K. Gibson-Graham (eds) *Making other worlds possible: Performing diverse economies*, Minneapolis, MN: University of Minnesota Press (www.jstor.org/stable/10.5749/j.ctt130jtq1.15).

Peck, J. (2008) 'Remaking laissez-faire', *Progress in Human Geography* 32(1), 3-43 (https://doi.org/10.1177/0309132507084816).

Peck, J. and Theodore, N. (2007) 'Variegated capitalism', *Progress in Human Geography* 31(6), 731-72 (https://doi.org/10.1177/0309132507083505).

Peck, J. and Theodore, N. (2010) 'Recombinant workfare, across the Americas: Transnationalizing "fast" social policy', *Geoforum* 41(2), 195-208.

Pellow, D.N. and Park, L. (2002) *The Silicon Valley of dreams: Environmental injustice, immigrant workers, and the high-tech global economy*, New York: New York University Press.

Pettinger, L. (2015) 'Embodied labour in music work: Embodied labour in music work', *The British Journal of Sociology*, 66(2), 282-300 (https://doi.org/10.1111/1468-4446.12123).

Pettinger, L., Parry, J., Taylor, R. and Glucksmann, M. (2005) *A new sociology of work?*, Oxford: Blackwell.

Phillips, N. and Mieres, F. (2015) 'The governance of forced labour in the global economy', *Globalizations* 12(2), 244-60 (https://doi.org/10.1080/14747731.2014.932507).

Pierce, J.L. (2012) *Racing for innocence: Whiteness, gender, and the backlash against affirmative action*, Stanford, CA: Stanford University Press.

Polanyi, M. (1966) *The tacit dimension*, New York, NY: Doubleday.

Portes, A., Castells, M. and Benton, L. (eds) (1989) *The informal economy: Studies in advanced and less developed countries*, Baltimore, MD: Johns Hopkins University Press.

Puig de la Bellacasa, M. (2017) *Matters of care: Speculative ethics in more than human worlds*, Minneapolis, MN: University of Minnesota Press.

Pulido, L. (2017) 'Geographies of race and ethnicity II: Environmental racism, racial capitalism and state-sanctioned violence', *Progress in Human Geography* 41(4), 524-33.

Rabinbach, A. (1990) *The human motor: Energy, fatigue, and the origins of modernity*, New York: Basic Books.

Reinecke, J., Donaghey, J., Wilkinson, A. and Wood, G. (2018) 'Global supply chains and social relations at work: Brokering across boundaries', *Human Relations* 71(4), 459-80.

Renner, M., Sweeney, S. and Kubit, J. (2008) *Green jobs: Towards decent work in a sustainable, low-carbon world*, Washington, DC: UNEP, ILO/IOE/ITUC, Worldwatch Institute.

Rifkin, J. (1995) *The end of work: The decline of the global labor force and the dawn of the post-market era*, New York: GP Putnam's Sons.

Robbins, P. (2007) 'Carbon colonies: From local use value to global exchange in 21st century postcolonial forestries', in S. Raju, S. Kumar and S. Corbridge (eds) *Colonial and postcolonial geographies of India*, London: Sage, pp 279-97.

Roelvink, G. (2015) 'Performing posthumanist economies in the Anthropocene', in K. St Martin, G. Roelvink and J.K. Gibson-Graham (eds) *Making other worlds possible: Performing diverse economies*, Minneapolis, MN: University of Minnesota Press, pp 225-43.

Rood, D. (2017) *The reinvention of Atlantic slavery: Technology, labor, race, and capitalism in the Greater Caribbean*, Oxford: Oxford University Press.

Ross, A. (1996) 'The future is a risky business', in G. Robertson, M. Mash, L. Tickner, J. Bird, B. Curtis and T. Putnam (eds) *FutureNatural: Nature, science, culture*, London: Routledge, pp 7-21.

Ross, A. (2008) 'The new geography of work: Power to the precarious?', *Theory, Culture and Society* 25(7-8), 31-49 (https://doi.org/10.1177/0263276408097795).

Roy, D. (1959) '"Banana time": Job satisfaction and informal interaction', *Human Organization* 18, 158-68.

Santos, B.S. (2004) 'A critique of lazy reason: Against the waste of experience', in I. Wallerstein (ed) *The modern world-system in the Longue Durée*, Boulder, CO: Paradigm Publishers, pp 157-97.

Scheiber, N. (2017) 'How Uber uses psychological tricks to push its drivers' buttons', *New York Times*, 2 April (www.nytimes.com/interactive/2017/04/02/technology/uber-drivers-psychological-tricks.html).

Schneider, F. (2016) *Estimating the size of the shadow economies of highly-developed countries: Selected new results*, CESifo DICE Report, ISSN 1613-6373, Munich: Leibniz-Institute for Economic research (IFO Institut) University of Munich 14(4), 44-53.

Schulz, J.M. (2015) 'Winding down the workday: Zoning the evening hours in Paris, Oslo, and San Francisco', *Qualitative Sociology* 38(3), 235-59 (https://doi.org/10.1007/s11133-015-9309-0).

Scott, J.C. (2012) *Two cheers for anarchism*, Princeton, NJ: Princeton University Press.

Sen, I. (2009) 'Colonial domesticities, contentious interactions: Ayahs, wet-nurses and memsahibs in Colonial India', *Indian Journal of Gender Studies* 16(3), 299-328 (https://doi.org/10.1177/097152150901600301).

Sennett, R. (2008) *The craftsman*, London: Penguin Books.

Sharma, S. (2014) *In the meantime: Temporality and cultural politics*, Durham, NC: Duke University Press.

Shestakofsky, B. (2017) 'Working algorithms: Software automation and the future of work', *Work and Occupations* 44(4), 376-423.

Siegmann, K.A. and Schiphorst, F. (2016) 'Understanding the globalizing precariat: From informal sector to precarious work', *Progress in Development Studies* 16(2), 111-23 (https://doi.org/10.1177/1464993415623118).

Silver, B.J. (2003) *Forces of labor: Workers' movements and globalization since 1870*, Cambridge and New York: Cambridge University Press.

Simone, A. (2015) 'Afterword, come out, you're surrounded. The between of infrastructure', *City* 19(2-3), 375-83.

Simone, A. and Fauzan, A.U. (2013) 'On the way to being middle class: The practices of emergence in Jakarta', *City* 17(3), 279-98.

Singh, N.M. (2013) 'The affective labor of growing forests and the becoming of environmental subjects: Rethinking environmentality in Odisha, India', *Geoforum* 47, 189-98.

Snell, D. and Fairbrother, P. (2013) 'Just transition and labour environmentalism in Australia', in N. Räthzel and D. Uzzell (eds) *Trade unions in the green economy: Working for the environment*, London: Routledge, pp 146-91.

Star, S.L. (1991) 'The sociology of the invisible: The primacy of work in the writings of Anselm Strauss', in D.R. Maines (ed) *Social organization and social process: Essays in honor of Anselm Strauss*, Hawthorne, NY: Aldine de Gryter, pp 265-83.

Star, S.L. (1992) 'The trojan door: Organizations, work, and the "open black box"', *Systemic Practice and Action Research* 5(4), 395-410.

Stengers, I. (2005) 'The cosmopolitical proposal', in B. Latour and P. Webel (eds) *Making things public*, Cambridge, MA: MIT Press, pp 994-1003.

Stengers, I. (2015) *In catastrophic times: Resisting the coming barbarism* (translated by A. Goffey), Lüneburg, Germany: Open Humanities Press/Meson Press.

Stengers, I. (2019: forthcoming) *The Virgin Mary and the Neutrino*, Durham, NC: Duke University Press.

Stengers, I. and Ralet, O. (1997) 'Drugs: Ethical choice or moral consensus', in I. Stengers (ed) *Power and invention: Situating science*, Minneapolis, MN: University of Minnesota Press.

Stevis, D. (2013) 'Green jobs? Good jobs? Just jobs?', in N. Räthzel and D. Uzzell (eds) *Trade unions in the green economy: Working for the environment*, London: Routledge, pp 179-95.

Strangleman, T. (2005) 'Sociological futures and the sociology of work', *Sociological Research Online* 10(4), 1-12.

Strasser, S. (1982) *Never done: A history of American housework*, New York: Pantheon.

Strathern, M. (2006) 'Bullet-proofing: A tale from the United Kingdom', in A. Riles (ed) *Documents: Artifacts of modern knowledge*, Ann Arbor, MI: University of Michigan Press, pp 181–205.

Strauss, A.L., Fagerhaugh, S., Suczek, B. and Wiener, C. (1985) *The social organization of medical work*, Chicago, IL: University of Chicago Press.

Streeck, W. (2016) *How will capitalism end? Essays on a failing system*, London: Verso.

Sullivan, F. and Wyatt, J. (2006) *ABC of health informatics*, Malden, MA: BMJ Books/Blackwell.

Taylor, R.F. (2004) 'Extending conceptual boundaries: Work, voluntary work and employment', *Work, Employment and Society* 18(1), 29–49 (https://doi.org/10.1177/0950017004040761).

Timmermans, S. and Epstein, S. (2010) 'A world of standards but not a standard world: Toward a sociology of standards and standardization', *Annual Review of Sociology* 36(1), 69–89 (https://doi.org/10.1146/annurev.soc.012809.102629).

Timms, J. (2012) 'Where responsibility lies: Corporate social responsibility and campaigns for the rights of workers in a global economy', Doctoral dissertation, London: London School of Economics and Political Science.

Tokatli, N. (2003) 'Globalization and the changing clothing industry in Turkey', *Environment and Planning A* 35(10), 1877–94 (https://doi.org/10.1068/a3632).

Trentmann, F. (2007) 'Before "fair trade": Empire, free trade, and the moral economies of food in the modern world', *Environment and Planning D: Society and Space* 25(6), 1079–102 (https://doi.org/10.1068/d448t).

Tsing, A. (2009) 'Supply chains and the human condition', *Rethinking Marxism* 21(2), 148–76.

Tsing, A.L. (2015) *The mushroom at the end of the world: On the possibility of life in capitalist ruins*, Princeton, NJ: Princeton University Press.

Urry, J. (2014) *Offshoring*, London: Polity.

Vail, M.I. (2018) *Liberalism in illiberal states: Ideas and economic adjustment in contemporary Europe*, Oxford: Oxford University Press.

Venugopal, R. (2015) 'Neoliberalism as concept', *Economy and Society* 44(2), 165-87.

Wajcman, J. (2006) 'New connections: Social studies of science and technology and studies of work', *Work, Employment and Society* 20(4), 773-86.

Wallerstein, I. (2004) *World-systems analysis: An introduction*, Durham, NC: Duke University Press.

Weeks, K. (2011) *The problem with work: Feminist, Marxist, antiwork politics, and postwork imaginaries*, Durham, NC and London: Duke University Press.

Wheeler, K. and Glucksmann, M. (2015) *Household recycling and consumption work: Social and moral economies*, Basingstoke: Palgrave Macmillan.

Whyte, W. (1946) 'When workers and customers meet', in W. Whyte (ed) *Industry and society*, New York: McGraw-Hill.

Widdows, H. and Smith, N. (eds) (2011) *Global social justice*, London: Routledge.

Williams, C. (2004) *Cash-in-hand work: The underground sector and the hidden economy of favours*, Basingstoke: Palgrave Macmillan.

Williams, C.C. (2006) 'Beyond market-oriented readings of paid informal work: Some lessons from rural England', *American Journal of Economics and Sociology* 65(2), 383-406 (https://doi.org/10.1111/j.1536-7150.2006.00455.x).

Williams, E. (1944) *Capitalism and slavery*, Chapel Hill and London: UNC Press Books, 1994.

Wolkowitz, C. (2006) *Bodies at work*, Thousand Oaks, CA: Sage.

World Bank, The (2018) *World development report draft 2019: The changing nature of work*, Washington, DC: The World Bank.

Index

References to pages with tables are in *italics*

225

Index